MY LIFE WITH THE JEDI

THE SPIRITUALITY OF STAR WARS

ERIC A. CLAYTON

LOYOLA PRESS.
A JESUIT MINISTRY

Chicago

There are many books analyzing the philosophical, religious, and mythical themes of the Star Wars saga, but Eric Clayton has provided us with something quite different—a *how-to* manual for living one's life according to the saga's lessons. In drawing connections between the wisdom of wise Jedi Masters and the *Spiritual Exercises* of St. Ignatius, this book teaches one how to become a contemplative in action, with or without a lightsaber or X-Wing.

Jason T. Eberl, Ph.D., co-editor of *Star Wars and Philosophy* and *Star Wars and Philosophy Strikes Back*, and director and professor of the Albert Gnaegi Center for Health Care Ethics, Saint Louis University

My Life with the Jedi is essential reading for *Star Wars* fans—especially those wishing to launch their love of *Star Wars* as a vehicle for self-discovery. Its treatment of *Star Wars* is thorough, with relevant examples from events and characters not just from the main saga but from *Star Wars* books, television, comics, even animated shorts. This diversity helps Clayton build his case that many spiritual lessons can be drawn from *Star Wars*—sometimes from unexpected parts of the galaxy far, far away. If you loved Matthew Bortolin's books (*The Dharma of Star Wars*, *The Zen of R2-D2*), you'll love *My Life With the Jedi*.

Emily Strand, M.A., instructor of Comparative Religions and Cultural Competence, Mount Carmel College; co-editor of *Star Wars: Essays Exploring a Galaxy Far, Far Away*

Even the newest fans of the now-classic Star Wars films will recognize often profound themes of good and evil, sin and redemption, and despair and hope. In his engaging and enlightening new book Eric Clayton reveals these hidden (and not so hidden) themes, and invites us to see how the Spirit, if not the Force, can lead us to make good and life-giving decisions.

Fr. James Martin, SJ, author of *My Life with the Saints*

A brilliant spin on *Star Wars* and spirituality; "This *is* how the Force works!" *My Life with the Jedi: The Spirituality of Star Wars* is a mindful and soulful journey between the monomyth and our luminous selves.

Becca Benjamin and Mark Sutter, *Tarkin's Top Shelf* Podcast

———⌐——————

It's no secret that the galaxies of Star Wars are suffused with spiritual force. In *My Life with the Jedi*, Eric Clayton does more than uncover the morals within the mythic stories. Blending Ignatian spirituality and a deep knowledge of Star Wars, he does what the best spiritual writers do: help us see ourselves and our lives in inspiring new ways.

Daniel Burke, former religion editor for CNN and Director of Communications at the Georgetown University Center on Faith and Justice

———⌐——————

For many of us, the stories and characters of Star Wars have served as spiritual companions through the years, offering us inspiration in times of trial, kinship when we've felt alone, consolation as we've grieved, and a mirror to reflect our truest selves back to us in the face of doubt and fear. In *My Life with the Jedi*, Eric Clayton honors those treasured experiences while simultaneously inviting us to consider new ways the series might usher us into a more examined life of faith. This is the book spiritually-minded Star Wars fans have been waiting for.

Shannon K. Evans, spirituality and culture editor of the *National Catholic Reporter*

———⌐——————

What do a sixteenth-century-Spanish-nobleman-turned-saint and a wrinkled green alien warrior-monk have in common? More than you might think! In *My Life with the Jedi*, Eric Clayton digs deep into the Star Wars saga, revealing how the characters and tales of a galaxy far, far away can help us find God in our everyday lives. Writing with clarity, compassion, and humor, Clayton weaves together Star Wars canon and wisdom from the Spiritual Exercises in ways that can be enjoyed by experts and casual fans alike.

John Dougherty, Director of Campus Ministry at St. Joseph's Prep; writer of "Catholic Movie Club" for *America Magazine*

LOYOLA PRESS.
A JESUIT MINISTRY

www.loyolapress.com

Cover art credit: Anastassiya Bezhekeneva/Moment/Getty Images, nevro2008/ iStock/Getty Images
Loyola Press Author photo: Allison Clayton

ISBN-13: 978-0-8294-5701-8
Library of Congress Control Number: 2023945727

Printed in the United States of America.
23 24 25 26 27 28 29 30 31 32 Versa 10 9 8 7 6 5 4 3 2 1

For Elianna and Camira:

May you never forget what luminous beings you are.

And hope does not disappoint.
—Romans 5:5

CONTENTS

INTRODUCTION: MYTH

I was roughly ten years old when I first saw *Star Wars*. My dad dusted off his VHS collection and popped *A New Hope* into the video player, and off we went to a galaxy far, far away. I was captivated by the adventures of Luke Skywalker.

In the days, weeks, and years that followed, I daydreamed about becoming a Jedi Knight. I waved my hand at the automatic doors at the grocery store. I swung empty wrapping paper tubes at my little brother. I said things like, "May the Force be with you." I bet I'm not the only one.

There's something about the mythos of Star Wars that goes beyond the telling of a good story. Star Wars is not just a tale of knights going off to battle, of bounty hunters pursuing dangerous quarries, of politicians waging diplomatic warfare. The story's mythos portrays the sense that the galaxy itself is so much bigger and more mysterious than we can possibly imagine. Some ancient wisdom is just out of sight. There is a power that is available to everyone, even though it is hidden, and it holds everything together. And we, in our very non-Jedi lives, actually have a role to play in all of this. There are mystical forces calling out to us, if we have the patience and wherewithal to look and listen closely.

And these powers? These forces? They affect not only the vastness of galactic history but also the personal stories buried within our very selves. Yes, the Force guides entire civilizations and is available to warriors as sword and sustenance. But the Force is also a deeply intimate well from which to draw individual strength.

Star Wars oozes spirituality. From movies to television, from books to comics, from video games to cosplaying, this ongoing multimedia, multigenerational mythic tale invites us to look inside ourselves, weigh the light and the dark found therein, and discover our own place in this great big galaxy. This is what a ten-year-old Jedi wannabe swinging a cardboard lightsaber was seeking: a deeper understanding of my own power, my own purpose. That's what I still seek—and again, I bet I'm not alone.

Yoda reminds us that we are luminous beings, more than just the crude matter we can see and touch. There's more to all of us and to our stories than meets the eye. The spiritual journey is essential to uncovering who we are and what our own luminous purpose truly is. But this is a journey not easily undertaken.

That's all right. We don't have to go it alone. And we shouldn't. Spirituality is not solely a personal thing; it necessarily brings us out of ourselves and into community. After all, as old Ben Kenobi explains in *A New Hope*, the Force is "an energy field created by all living things. . . . It binds the galaxy together." Our purpose is bound up in the purposes of others. Our place in this galaxy can be understood only by striving to understand who and what is here with us.

A MYTHIC FORCE IN EACH OF US

Throughout this book, I hope to be your companion on this journey—no matter what spiritual tradition, if any, you claim. George Lucas, the creator of Star Wars, was a student of Joseph Campbell's work on comparative religions and mythologies. Campbell saw mythology as a provider of symbols and rituals meant to "carry the human spirit forward."[1] It's no wonder Lucas wanted folks to find themselves in and be challenged by the story—*and spirituality*—of Star Wars. As journalist Chris Taylor writes in his seminal book *How Star Wars Conquered the Universe*, "The Force is so basic a concept as to be universally appealing: a religion for the secular age that is so well suited to our times precisely because it is so bereft of detail. Everyone gets to add their own layers of meaning."[2] Everyone gets to see their own spiritual journey reflected back to them through Star Wars.

As we explore the spiritual resonance that this epic space fantasy has in our own lives, I hope you will discover and embrace layers of meaning from the story that are uniquely your own.

But first, let me share the layers of meaning that *I* hope to contribute. I am a Catholic and a student of Ignatian spirituality. St. Ignatius of Loyola was a soldier-turned-mystic who was born in the Basque region of Spain in the final years of the fifteenth century.[3] One of his primary insights into the spiritual life, something that is foundational to the spiritual tradition that bears his name to this day, is the awareness that *God is in all things*. In other words, there is a spark of the divine in each of us, and the holy and the sacred abound everywhere. The world is literally dripping with grace. We all are made of God-stuff.

Thinking back to Yoda's and Obi-Wan's definitions of the Force as an invitation to consider all things as interconnected and pulsing with sacred energy has led me to believe that Ignatian spirituality is a powerful way to approach and unpack the spirituality of Star Wars. And so, throughout the three parts of this book, I will highlight key Ignatian spiritual principles that will help us use characters, places, and themes from Star Wars to make sense of our own spiritual lives.

Part 1, "Naming the Phantom Menace," is an examination of both the forces in our lives that prevent us from embracing new spiritual opportunities, and the forces that might be beckoning us onward, but go unheard. We will talk about how

- our deepest desires help us respond to the call of adventure;
- a change in focus awakens us to new potential;
- our inevitable woundedness is something to be embraced; and
- we recognize and respond to social structures that perpetuate injustice.

The second part, "Engaging the Duel of the Fates," brings the collision of spiritual forces deep into our inner lives. We will reflect on

- the dark side caves in our own lives that keep us trapped in shame and fear;

- two distinct Ignatian principles for discerning next steps, no matter where we are in our spiritual journeys; and
- what Ignatius called the Two Standards, which is a meditation that could have been pulled right from the pages of Lucas's Star Wars scripts, as it helps us uncover why the dark side is so seductive.

In the final part, "Discerning a New Hope," we explore the needs of our communities. We bring our own spirituality into conversation with the spirituality of others, plotting ways in which we can better serve the common good and the needs of our world. To do this, we

- reflect on how an astromech droid exemplifies the Ignatian practice of indifference;
- learn from the Jedi Order as we examine the role of institutions in the spiritual life;
- explore the importance of redemption in Star Wars and consider the role it plays in our own lives; and
- unpack what it means to be a pilgrim, and what the lifestyle of a Mandalorian bounty hunter might have to teach us.

In addition to Ignatian spirituality, I will be sharing insights from other spiritual traditions I have found useful in my spiritual life, as well as the occasional story from my own epic Star Wars adventures.

Each chapter will conclude with a "Wayfinder Exercise," an invitation for you to meditate on *your* story. These exercises are based on what Ignatius of Loyola called the *examen*. The *examen* is a prayer of gratitude that invites us to recognize that the most ordinary moments of every day contain sacred potential. Why call them Wayfinder Exercises? In a galaxy far away, wayfinders are pyramidal artifacts that fit in the palm of your hand and contain navigational secrets. We saw in *The Rise of Skywalker* that Kylo Ren needed a wayfinder to plot his path to Exegol. And while our Wayfinder Exercises hopefully will not land us on a planet of hooded Sith acolytes, they *will* help us reflect on where we've been so that we can plot our way forward more intentionally.

OUR CERTAIN POINTS OF VIEW

I'll wager a guess that if you're reading this book, you both love Star Wars and are intrigued by the spiritual insights this great myth can bring to your life. I hope, too, that you're open to being challenged because the spiritual journey takes you deep within yourself and, in so doing, also plunges you deep within the beating heart of the universe. Language can often fall short of the mysteries we're trying to understand. As Harvard professor Cass Sunstein writes in his wonderful book *The World according to Star Wars*, "*Star Wars* doesn't tell you what to think. It invites speculation. You can understand it in different, even contradictory ways."[4] He's right. It depends on your (certain) point of view.

For someone who prefers a spiritual journey with clear guideposts, all this potential for contradiction and nuance might be unsettling. I find these words from the great Franciscan mystic Fr. Richard Rohr, written in his book *The Universal Christ*, deeply consoling: "Just because you do not have the right word for God does not mean you are not having the right experience. From the beginning, YHWH let the Jewish people know that no right word would ever contain

God's infinite mystery. . . . Controlling people try to control people, and they do the same with God—but loving anything always means a certain giving up of control."[5]

Jedi are warned against holding too tightly to any one thing, any one person, any one idea. For Jedi and for us, there is a need to surrender expectations, prejudices, and control. It's not easy—but we have a whole book with which to practice.

Now, this is where the fun begins.

PART 1

NAMING THE PHANTOM MENACE

It was 1999 and I was in fourth grade when *The Phantom Menace* premiered in theaters. My friends and I had spent the months leading up to the release date studying whatever information we could get our hands on: magazine stories, interviews, movie reviews, even a few tidbits on the fledgling Internet. So much about the movie was unknown; there was so much to be excited about.

The mysterious Sith Lord, Darth Sidious, was chief among the mysteries we sought to unravel. Who was this character? What was he after? He looked a lot like another villain from the original trilogy.

Even to a fourth grader, it should have been obvious. Darth Sidious *is* Senator-turned-Chancellor Palpatine. He's *also* who we would come to know as Emperor Palpatine. And, more than twenty years later, he is the mastermind of the Sith Eternal. That eerie blue hologram of a hooded figure cloaked in shadow was pretty consistent with what we saw in *The Empire Strikes Back*. Unsurprisingly, it was actor Ian McDiarmid who played all three iterations.

But for whatever reason, I would not see the obvious. I spent weeks trying to convince my friends that these were different people, that Darth Sidious couldn't be Emperor Palpatine, if for no other reason than that it *was* too obvious. And Senator Palpatine? To me, these were different characters doing different things.

A phantom menace, indeed.

We all have moments like this. Moments when we couldn't—or *wouldn't*—see what was clearly right in front of us. Take a minute now to name such a time in your life. What was it? How did this blindness—willful or otherwise—impact you? Things that seem so apparent in retrospect can often be veiled in the moment. We may be *unable* to see what's right there at our fingertips, or we may be *unwilling* to see it. Either way, it's okay. The spiritual life is one built on discernment. On understanding our own biases and limitations, our own strengths and insights. And on making decisions accordingly.

The literal phantom menace of the Star Wars universe turned out to be a corrupt Lord of the Sith. But such phantoms need not be evil to wreak havoc in our lives. Often, those phantoms are the things gnawing away at the edges of our mind, pushing and pulling us in directions we don't yet understand or see clearly, all the while keeping us up at night. There is very likely a lot of good to be had in discerning these phantom spirits, but discernment takes work, and that work can be difficult. That's what the first part of this book is all about: *naming* the phantom menaces in our spiritual life, *understanding* what they are, and *figuring out* where they might be pushing us to go—or what they might be holding us back from.

Our goal here is to learn from the mistakes of my fourth-grade self. The point is to look directly and unflinchingly at the spiritual menaces that wake us in the dead of night and affect our day-to-day. Let's call them what they are. When we do, we'll be able to sink into the spiritual life in a deeper, more meaningful way, and grapple with life in all its nuance, beauty, and wonder.

CHAPTER 1

SAND

Anakin Skywalker famously dislikes sand. "It's coarse and rough and irritating," he says. The line is stilted and silly and justifiably infamous. But despite our hero's distaste for sand, planets made from the stuff do seem to produce an abundance of Star Wars protagonists. The journeys of Anakin, Luke, and Rey all begin on desert planets. Tatooine itself plays an outsized role in the saga. How many times can our characters return to the twin-sunned planet? Obi-Wan Kenobi, Ezra Bridger, Din Djarin, Boba Fett—it seems as though no heroic arc is complete without getting a bit of sand in your boots. And the planet Jakku plays a similarly hefty role for many of the heroes and villains of the stories released in tandem with the sequel trilogy.

It's easy to dismiss all these sandy planets as nods to the fans or lazy storytelling. But what if there's more here? More to what we're meant to learn from that coarse, rough, irritating stuff?

At best, sand is uncomfortable. And that's exactly where spiritual journeys begin: with discomfort. We get the sinking suspicion that something is not quite right, that there's more here than meets the eye. That perhaps we're called to something greater than what we can see or feel or touch or taste. *But what might it be? And how do we get there?* Questions we'll reflect on in this chapter.

That spiritual sand grating on our very lives demands a response. It demands action, adventure, sacrifice, self-discovery. Perhaps our heroes begin their quests in sandy places for this same reason: The sand is *meant* to make them uncomfortable so that they get about the business of answering the questions that matter. Am I *really* meant to become a Jedi? Am I *really* meant to save the princess? Am I *really* able to be part of the Resistance?

In our spiritual lives, the questions look a little different, but they point in the same direction: Who are we meant to become? What's driving us? It might seem safe to stay where it's mentally comfortable and ignore risky questions. But really, it's dangerous. We shouldn't suppress or ignore the person we are meant to be. It's the spiritual sand that goads us forward.

DISCOVERING DEEP DESIRES

The goal of Ignatian spirituality is to help individuals and communities discover their deepest desires so that they can discern their life's purpose. Ignatius of Loyola's *Spiritual Exercises* are foundational to this effort, and will be our guide. The Exercises are a distillation of Ignatius's own spiritual journey. Though each of us has a unique path before us, Ignatius realized that there are similarities between and parallels within our spiritual lives.

At the outset, Ignatius provides a short introductory note called the First Principle and Foundation. Its purpose is to set the stage for all that is to come and encourage the seeker to assume a disposition of openness to the work of the Spirit in his or her life. Ignatius writes, "Our one desire and choice should be what is more conducive to the end for which we are created."

Is a Catholic saint suggesting we explore and act upon our *desires*? Absolutely! Ignatius believed that our deepest desires reflected God's dream for us, that buried in those desires were holy seeds planted by the Spirit. Desires are not meant to be suppressed; rather, they are meant to be understood, held up to the light and inspected, and then acted upon. We *need* to know what it is we feel uniquely called to *do*—and *why*. What we're passionate about, what excites or disgusts us, what makes us angry or joyful or what stirs us to tears—these are *essential* breadcrumbs that lead us deeper into ourselves.

Obviously, not *every* desire leads us somewhere good. Sometimes, after careful reflection, we discover that a particular desire is leading us astray. Cheating on a romantic partner, for example, might be a desire, but it's likely one that, once understood, we know to resist. Too often, though, we're tempted to look at our desires superficially. We stop at our desire for sex rather than wonder if that desire is leading us deeper into a particular relationship. We stop at our desire for wealth or fame rather than wonder if those desires are inviting us to consider how we might use our resources for the good of others. We stop at our desire for a job rather than think about how a certain set of skills or experiences brings us deep satisfaction. And the desire to cheat on a partner? That, too, is probably pointing somewhere: perhaps to a desire for deeper intimacy, or personal freedom, or the need to mend inner wounds.

Returning to the First Principle and Foundation, it's helpful to highlight the Jesuit concept of *magis*. Simply put, *magis* means "more." But not more in the sense that you're acquiring additional stuff or greater influence or an elevated reputation; rather, how can I—how can you—live out that purpose or vocation that only we can manifest in this world for the greater good? How can we become more authentically who we are meant to be? How can we become more authentically ourselves?

Our experience, insights, and passions make up the unique people that we are. We look carefully at our desires because they have the potential to set us on a unique, essential path. We talk about the will of God. In truth, discovering and acting upon our deepest desires—who we are meant to be—is *the same thing* as discovering and acting upon the will of God.

But it's not easy. There are plenty of temptations along the way. Sometimes, we need a little discomfort to stir us to action.

WHAT HOLDS US BACK

A young Anakin Skywalker, upon meeting Padmé Amidala in Watto's junk shop, claims to be a pilot. He insists that one day he'll fly away from Tatooine, where, as a slave, he's been bound all his life. Of *course* he wants to leave it behind. He bristles when Padmé is dismissive of him, a mere slave, and retorts that he's a person and has a name. We glimpse a boy who dreams of something beyond the junkyard, beyond the sand, beyond even the thrill of podracing—and yet he cannot really envision what a different life might look like.

Because this is all he's ever known, when the Jedi Master Qui-Gon Jinn gives Anakin the chance to leave Tatooine and train as a Jedi, he hesitates. Is he ready—is he *able*—to leave his life behind? To leave his mother, Shmi? To embrace a new life as a Jedi? For all his talk, young Anakin is not so sure.

A generation later, Anakin's son, Luke, is also itching to leave Tatooine. Luke wants to enroll in the Imperial Academy, clearly an act of desperation to get away from the monotony of moisture farming. He's frustrated with the rules and limitations imposed by his uncle, Owen Lars.

But he, too, gets cold feet when the opportunity to leave presents itself. In a deleted scene from *A New Hope*, Luke reunites with his old friend Biggs Darklighter at Tosche Station. Biggs presses Luke on his upcoming entrance into the Academy, encouraging him to use it as a jumping off point to join the Rebel Alliance. But Luke is suddenly reluctant. Biggs is frustrated to hear that Luke is postponing his entrance. Luke insists he can't leave his uncle now; he's needed around the Lars homestead. It appears that Luke doesn't want rules and restrictions . . . until he does.

And Rey: All her life she looks to the skies above Jakku, hoping, yearning to see some sign that her parents are returning to her. She counts the days, marking one after another in her abandoned AT-AT-turned home. Does she want to go after them? Does she want to take her destiny into her own hands rather than continue scavenging for junk? When the spunky droid BB-8 rolls into her life, quickly followed by the mysterious stormtrooper-turned-Resistance-hero Finn, she has her chance. It's Rey who saves them all, who gets that old pile of junk, the *Millennium Falcon*, into the air. She enables her new crew to escape the First Order TIE Fighters that are pursuing them. But once the thrill of the moment is over, she tells Finn she has to get back to Jakku and her humdrum life of scavenging. An exasperated Finn can't fathom why anyone would want to return to such a place.

Why, indeed? Each of our heroes knew what they wanted—they'd said as much. They knew what got them out of bed in the morning. And yet, when the time came to act, they faltered. The inability to claim what we really desire, even after having recognized and named it, isn't a spiritual phenomenon bound only to a galaxy far, far away. We here on Earth feel it, too.

It's fear. We're afraid. Better to accommodate the irritation of the sand than to step into the unknown. We're afraid of falling short. We fear the sting of shame, proof that we aren't who we thought we were, and that maybe this really is it. We're afraid that the status quo is all we'll ever get, so we commit to uphold it rather than cast it aside.

Here's an antidote: We need to foster a belief in ourselves that anchors us to one another. We need to cultivate belief that transcends who we are as individuals and necessarily puts us on a collision course with the needs of others.

THE BOOK OF BOBA'S FEARS

Allow me to stretch this sand metaphor about as far as it will go. Remember Boba Fett? The sand literally *ate* him. (Well, actually, the sarlacc did, but you get my meaning.) Desires that are suppressed and ignored? They don't go away. They eat you up.

What brought Boba Fett to the Great Pit of Carkoon? A desire for money and reputation. He was a bounty hunter, after all. But he wanted more; his *deepest* desires weren't for wealth and fame. As we saw in *The Book of Boba Fett*, he longed for connection, for purpose, for community. And he missed his father. None of that got sorted out though before he got on Jabba's sail barge. And so, the sand—his unfulfilled desires—consumed him.

But his story doesn't end there. Trapped by all that grating sand, Fett decided he wasn't done living. Desires had gone unfulfilled; his true purpose had not been discovered. And he refused to let all those missed opportunities, all those tiny grains of sand, collapse in on him and destroy him. That gloved fist punches back into the Tatooine sun, and his adventures continue. This is the beauty of the spiritual life: it keeps unfolding. The path ends only when we stop walking.

However, like many things in our spiritual lives, sand can cause both consolation and desolation. Context is everything. So it is that in the second episode of *The Book of Boba Fett*, when Boba Fett wanders into the desert of Tatooine (clearly high off of some mystical Tusken lizard), the sand acts as a purifier. The very discomfort is what beckons him forward. The vision he finds in that sea of sand brings him some peace, consolation, and a deeper understanding of himself and his new life. It washes away something of his past so that he can look to his future.

Boba returns to the Tusken Raiders, who then equip him with the tools to survive and thrive in the harsh environment of Tatooine. (Thankfully, they also reclaim the lizard.) He now has a community, a belief in himself, and people to whom he feels anchored. And even when that community is taken from him, he is able to cling to his renewed sense of purpose, and he finds others with whom he can share it. His work is not yet done. He wants more. He wants the *magis*. The sand did its job.

NOW DIG DEEP

When it comes to sand, we have to dig deep if we want to get anywhere, lest it all keep falling back in on itself. (All right, that's the last of my sand analogies—I promise.) But if we want to *sustain* our response to this call to adventure, we must ask—and try to answer—hard questions. Even if we have a sense of what we really want and what these desires are pointing us toward, if we're going to ride out the inevitable challenges and struggles that will come our way, we must know not only what path we are on but also why we're on it. Because the excitement and sense of adventure fade. And when they do, what will sustain us when we round the proverbial Death Star corner and come face-to-face with dozens of angry stormtroopers?

Think back to our sandy Star Wars heroes. Did Anakin *really* just want to be a pilot? Well, yes, in part (just like part of his motivation was to get close to Padmé). But at its core, the great desire of this child-slave was the yearning to play a bigger role in a galaxy that had seemingly forgotten him. Simply put, he wanted to help other people. He also wanted to experience a relationship that wasn't defined by mere financial incentives. He dreamed of creating a family built on the love and trust that had been so rare in his own childhood. Luke didn't just want to escape Tatooine, or even join the Academy. He wanted to find his place in the galaxy and discover what it was that was calling to him beyond the sands of his childhood. Biggs touched a nerve when he mentioned the Rebel Alliance, an organization that didn't just go along to get along—much as Luke had his entire life. Was this what the future Jedi was yearning for? A way to break past the rules and restrictions imposed on him by his uncle in a way that made a meaningful difference in the galaxy?

And Rey wanted her parents back; her desire was to belong to a family. But she was stuck on the idea that the concept of family had to pick up where it left off. She didn't have the inner freedom to see how her dream could be fulfilled anywhere but in the scrapyard of Jakku. And so, she had to allow herself to change and grow. She needed to leave Jakku and find purpose far beyond its sands and salvage. There she would find a new kind of family.

These things—authentic relationships, deeper meaning, family, and purpose—are the greater desires, our personal *magis* guideposts, that lead us out into our own galaxy. They give us a spiritual itch that demands our attention, demands our committed action.

The question we have to ask ourselves is actually twofold: *What do I really want, and why?* As soon as we ask that second question, we begin to uncover our values: what we believe about ourselves and our world.

What we learn from Luke, Anakin, Rey, and even Boba Fett is that our spiritual journey takes place in more than one dimension and on more than one level. We begin by tuning in to the call for change: I want something different. But when we keep digging, when we struggle to discover what's at the root of our desire, we uncover something deeper. We uncover what Ignatius says is God's desire for us.

This is when we realize that the change we seek is something profound, something within ourselves. It's not just a new job or a return to the way things once were. We don't just want to be pilot starfighters; we want to be pilot starfighters so as to protect planets that are under attack by oppressive regimes like the Trade Federation. We don't just want to join the Imperial Academy; we want to make our mark on a galaxy that is far bigger than we've ever imagined. We don't just want to have our old family life back; we want to live out new relationships here, now, in the present—even if that means excavating hard truths and working through trauma.

What do *you* really want? And why?

EVERYWHERE, SAND

1. **Reach out.** Extend a hand or simply your intentions toward the Holy Spirit. Do you feel it? Do you sense the permeability, the thinness of the veil that separates the physical and spiritual worlds? Center yourself in that place.

   Now, remaining in this place, bring to mind those tiny grains of sand that irritate or disrupt or distract.

2. **Set your intention.** What do you desire to be made known to you in this time, this space? What are those tiny grains of sand attempting to reveal about your life, your purpose, your destiny, your place in all of this?

Make your mantra by completing this sentence: *The sands in my life reveal* . . . what? Repeat that mantra several times. Be mindful of your breath.

3. **Review the past.** As you repeat your mantra, allow your mind to wander. Where does it go? Are you thinking of a moment from earlier today, earlier this year, or many years ago? Where do you see those grains of sand present? Where are they pushing you? Do you detect any patterns?

   Settle on a single moment. What questions does this moment raise in you? What excitement, fear, hope, or anxiety?

4. **Always in motion.** The moment you've settled on from your past necessarily informs your present and might guide you into the future. Do the same grains of sand blow now, in the present, compelling you to respond? Or is there something to be learned from your previous response that might inform some next step in the here and now?

5. **This is the way.** Informed by your reflection, commit to some small action you can take in the near future. What is it? What will it require? How might it affect the trajectory of your life?

End your reflection by cultivating a disposition of gratitude to yourself, the universe, and the infinite Other.

CHAPTER 2

FOCUS

When Luke shows up on the Dagobah doorstep of exiled Jedi Master Yoda, the small green Jedi quickly sizes him up: "All his life . . . never his mind on where he was," he laments in *The Empire Strikes Back*. Young Skywalker is never present to the moment. His whole life he's been dreaming about being somewhere else, doing something else. His mind is never in the here and now, never focused on what he's actually doing. And in this moment, Luke is hardly pleased to be wasting time on a swamp planet like Dagobah!

I wonder how many of us can relate to Luke: *I just need to accomplish the next great thing to find happiness!* I wonder how many of us can relate to Yoda: *But you're missing the greatness of life that is present right here, right now.* In each of us, I bet, there's a little of both.

In this chapter, we'll reflect on where we place our focus, and why it matters. The Ignatian tradition invites us to be contemplatives in action, which means that we are both mindful of the present moment and its potential as well as what we uniquely can contribute to shape it. It all starts with cultivating a deep sense of awareness of and gratitude for *the now*. When we sink into the nitty-gritty reality of our actual existence, we encounter the sacred. This is where we find the Holy, which is present in *all* things.

SWAMP LESSONS

On Dagobah, Yoda is teaching young Luke Skywalker the ways of the Force—and accusing him of always looking elsewhere for fulfillment and purpose. But who can blame Luke? Galactic history is chock full of powerful Force wielders casting their shadows over the Jedi-in-training. Surely, Luke feels the pressure. He's anxious to learn, to grow in power. Not so long ago he was nothing but a humble moisture farmer, so quite naturally he wants to prove he's more than that now. His driving motivation—and the thing that trips him up—is his desire to help his friends, to save them from the wrath of Darth Vader and the Empire. He wants to move fast. We can understand why Luke might quickly grow frustrated mucking about in the Dagobah swamps.

He's distracted by what he thinks to be important; what he believes to be "really" important is not the thing that Yoda is having him do. His mind busily envisions upcoming battles, and he concerns himself with worries about the fate of his friends, the outcome of the Rebellion, on what he might be called to do, and whether or not he'll be able to do it.

"Yoda tells Luke that he has spent his entire life looking to the future," observes Matthew Bortolin in his book *The Dharma of Star Wars*. Bortolin writes that the future is "that place beyond the horizon where we believe happiness exists—once we finish with this or achieve that."[6] Bortolin offers helpful insights from his own Buddhist tradition: "Mindfulness and concentration are a wake-up call to . . . come back to the only place we can live life and experience happiness—right now."[7] Practicing mindfulness can be understood as paying attention to both what is going on inside of us and outside of us by expanding our awareness so as to more readily notice what truly matters *in this moment*.

That's a hard pill to swallow when we are so frequently caught up in the anxiety of life: planning for the next meeting, the next class, the next summer camp, the next competition, or the next date. We are so often swept up in questions about what comes next—questions we struggle to answer, questions that consume us—that we find it all but impossible to simply sit and *be*. Rest is such a waste of time, right? Society affirms those who are prepared and scolds those caught wanting. If I can't be answering questions, tackling problems, preparing for whatever comes next, then what am I even *doing*?

The answer, of course, is *nothing*. And that's all right. That's actually *good*. Sometimes the *best* thing we can do is nothing. Stop the planning. Stop the jockeying. Stop the worrying. Jesus himself says "Do not worry" in his Sermon on the Mount. All the mind stuff—the chatter that mindfulness strives to quiet—prevents us from appreciating the beauty of everyday life. From gazing upon the universe with awe. Though mindfulness is often misunderstood as some kind of esoteric process, it's really just a way of settling into the *now*.

Luke found himself burdened by questions while training on Dagobah. Understandable. He wanted to absorb as much information as quickly as possible. Why not get a few questions answered about the nature of the dark side while swinging from those swampy vines? A Jedi's got to multitask, right? Again, Luke didn't want to be caught unprepared. But in trying to live in a potential future moment, he missed the real point of what Yoda was trying to teach him: focus on what you are doing now. When Luke's mind wanders too far from the present and he starts asking questions and being distracted, Yoda ends the training session. As Bortolin notes, "Yoda is inviting Luke to leave behind the world of questions, concepts and ideas, and return to the direct experience of life."[8]

There is a prayer by French Jesuit Pierre Teilhard de Chardin, SJ, that I return to often (see page 215). The prayer is an invitation to "trust in the slow work of God. We are quite naturally impatient in everything to reach the end without delay," de Chardin writes. "We are impatient of being on the way to something unknown, something new." We must allow ourselves to be shaped "without undue haste;" we cannot rush to the finish line without sinking into the graces of the present. De Chardin advises that we "accept the anxiety of feeling [ourselves] in suspense and incomplete."[9] In other words, we have to allow the universe and our experience of it to unfold in its own time. When we simply sit in the present moment to observe and watch and note all that is happening, we can glimpse the larger picture and see where we might be called. Perhaps, we might even discern the still, quiet voice of God.

In *The Phantom Menace*, Qui-Gon Jinn advises his young Padawan, Obi-Wan Kenobi, not to focus on his anxieties. He tells him to keep his concentration on the present, on the here and now. Kenobi is confused. The younger Jedi notes that it's Yoda himself who teaches the younglings to be mindful of the future. "But not at the expense of the moment," Qui-Gon counters.

Within each moment lies what we need to fashion the future we most desire—the future we hope to build, to be part of, to dream into existence for the good of all.

CONTEMPLATE, ACT, REVERSE, REPEAT

The Ignatian tradition invites us to be contemplatives in action. What this means is that our everyday experiences inform our prayer, and the fruits of our prayer inform our everyday experiences. Every moment of every day, every task or time in quiet reflection can be an instance of prayer. And those prayerful moments inform our daily activity. It's cyclical.

"What unites us to God is the practice of love. If prayer, or any other religious act, is not grounded in that, it is an offense to God,"[10] writes the late Jesuit priest Dean Brackley in his essential work *A Call to Discernment in Troubled Times*. Brackley lived and worked in El Salvador in the years following the 1989 assassination of his fellow Jesuits by the Salvadoran government. Spending years fighting for justice among those struggling in poverty, Brackley knew what it meant to allow his prayer to inform his experience, and his experience to inform his prayer. "If we are seeking to do God's will we are no less united to God in busy confusion than in formal prayer."[11]

We sift through the raw material of our everyday lives, searching for where the Spirit is at work and for opportunities to act on behalf of the common good. We observe, then act. But if we don't first sink into the present moment—that is, become *mindful* of what is actually going on and free ourselves from distracting anxieties and biases—we risk missing important, tiny details that can alter our lives and those of others.

Contemplation in action invites us to collaborate in the ongoing work of creation, in the building up of societies and the safeguarding of our universe. The very nature of *acting* upon our unique *contemplative practice* points to an important truth: our experiences matter and should be used to inform how we behave in the world—what we do and why we do it.

FOCUS DETERMINES REALITY

Qui-Gon Jinn tells a young Anakin Skywalker that his focus can determine his reality. That almost sounds like a magic trick, some self-helpy way to think our way into a better life. But it's true in this galaxy as well as in one that is (or was) far, far away.

Think about where you place your focus, what holds your attention. Whatever it is—a job, a set of values, family, friends, a personal dream—it takes up a lot of your time. It probably directs how you spend your days, your weeks, your months. How you spend your money, too. It's probably something you consult—a touchstone of sorts—before making a big life change.

But what if your focus goes beyond yourself? You want to work toward a more just world in which children don't go to bed hungry. You've lived in a town affected by food insecurity; you've seen the long-lasting impact hunger and a lack of nutrition can have on individuals and an entire community alike. You've lived this; you've heard the stories. Your focus, now, takes you on a vocational path that demands you advocate for legislation that helps feed the hungry as well as reimagine the entire global food chain. You yourself no longer waste food. As a result, neither does your family. And so on and so on.

This, too, is a way of allowing your focus to determine your reality, to really *see* what is right there in front of you—to observe it mindfully—and then act in a way that furthers the common good. Allowing your focus to determine the reality you hope to coexist within is another way of practicing contemplation in action.

And it necessarily brings you beyond yourself. The more you *observe* how your lived experience interacts with that of someone else, the more you truly *see* the other person. Jesuit priest Walter Burghardt says this kind of contemplation means taking "a long, loving look at the real."

> From such contemplation comes communion . . . the discovery of the Holy in deep, thoughtful encounters—with God's creation, with God's people, with God's self—where love is proven by sacrifice, the wild exchange of all for another, for the Other.[12]

Throughout history, some religious folks have been accused of turning a blind, impassive eye toward injustices, claiming that whatever is suffered in the present will pale in comparison to whatever will be enjoyed in the afterlife. That approach is woefully insufficient from the practical perspective of a contemplative in action. What we *gaze upon* now demands *action* now; it's an opportunity to manifest that love—a God who *is* love—that is essential to the spiritual life. We don't hold love back; we give it freely. That's what it means to integrate our contemplative life with our active life. It's a recognition that there is something holy and sacred that deserves deep, careful attention going on in each and every person. If we fail to give one another that attention, we risk missing the divine at work in our daily lives.

Our focus determines our reality. That's not a passive statement; it's a challenge to take a long, loving look at the world and allow ourselves to be moved by what we see.

"What you are in love with, what seizes your imagination, will affect everything," writes Joseph Whelan, SJ, in a famous prayer titled "Falling in Love."

> It will decide what will get you out of bed in the morning, what you do with your evenings, how you spend your weekends, what you read, whom you know, what breaks your heart, and what amazes you with joy and gratitude. Fall in Love, stay in love, and it will decide everything.[13]

PERHAPS IT IS TIME TO REFOCUS (AGAIN)

Professor Huyang, the delightfully sassy architect droid, has been training Jedi younglings in how to construct and wield lightsabers for more than 25,000 years. So in the second episode of *Ahsoka*, when he tells Sabine Wren that she's the *least* apt Force wielder he's ever encountered, he's really saying something. Sabine has no natural talent with the Force. She's a Mandalorian, after all—a historic *enemy* of the Jedi. And yet, Ahsoka Tano took her on, for better or worse, as her Padawan.

Even so, when Sabine is ready to give up, Huyang gives back her lightsaber and encourages her to begin again. Sabine, it seems, is too focused on what she *lacks*. She doesn't have the skill level of other Jedi; she can't connect to the Force. She can't live up to Ezra's legacy. She has disappointed Ahsoka.

She has failed her own Mandalorian people by surviving when they perished. As a result, her Mandalorian armor sits on a shelf and her lightsaber skills have grown rusty. Even so, perhaps because Sabine has been directing her focus to all the wrong things, Huyang tells her to begin again.

How often do we focus solely on what we lack, where we fall short, those things that seem impossible to accomplish—particularly when we compare ourselves to someone else? We enter in through the gateway of self-doubt and deficiency and are hardly surprised when we sputter and stall and are unable to muster the determination to continue.

Instead, we change our focus. We see ourselves through what we uniquely possess; we enter our story through the gateway of strengths and giftedness. Sabine's Mandalorian training was one of her greatest assets—and a unique set at that, compared to nearly every other Jedi. She was one of the few Mandalorians to ever wield the fabled Darksaber, and she learned how to do so under the tutelage of her friend and Jedi, Kanan Jarrus.

Of course, her Mandalorian training is not where her story ends. Huyang and Ahsoka are clear that she needs to continue growing, developing, and working on her connection to the Force. But focusing on her uniqueness as a Mandalorian, her own history and upbringing and set of experiences, is a much more productive way *into* her new spiritual journey. In this way, she is able to celebrate who she is rather than mourn all she is not.

And by changing her focus, by celebrating her strengths, she finds herself able to embrace the fullness of herself, leave the planet Lothal and what has become something of a self-imposed exile, and return to meeting the needs of the wider galaxy.

Contemplate who you've been, where you've been, and how those essential details have formed you for the present. Embrace them, and go forth.

ALWAYS A BIGGER FISH

Let's consider one more lesson on focus from Qui-Gon Jinn.

Along with Jar Jar Binks and Obi-Wan Kenobi, Qui-Gon is racing through the waters of Naboo in a bongo submarine, trying to reach the royal palace in time to save the queen. Jar Jar is a bit anxious; he's anticipating death by any number of underwater monsters, and he's quite vocal about his fears. When a big ol' fish monster does appear, Jar Jar freaks out. But Qui-Gon remains untroubled while Obi-Wan pilots the bongo onward. It's not long before their pursuer becomes prey to a different underwater creature.

"There's always a bigger fish," Qui-Gon observes.

In truth, there really wasn't much Qui-Gon, Obi-Wan, or Jar Jar *could* do in response to the appearance of that first fish. They just needed to keep doing what they were already doing and trust that it was enough. Keep the literal and figurative ship moving forward; don't allow panic to distract you. Focus on what is happening now—and on what you can realistically do in response. Accept those necessary limitations.

When the bongo loses power, Jar Jar is dismayed. Qui-Gon assures him that they're not in trouble yet. But Jar Jar is not having it. If not now, then when *would* they consider themselves in trouble? There are monsters within and without, and our heroes appear to be helpless.

But a simple rewiring of the vessel's power by Obi-Wan is all it takes before they're off again. Focus, presence, calm—these things allowed the slight course correction that was necessary to keep the bongo on track.

In our lives, there *are* always bigger fish: bigger threats, bigger goals, bigger problems, bigger successes. We imagine a moment of chaos cannot possibly get any worse—and then it does. Or we assume we've reached our personal or professional peak—until we realize there's a new goal we need to strive toward.

We can live in constant fear of the bigger fish. Or we can live in the moment. The bigger fish will exist regardless. We need not let them control our lives.

Instead, we can stay here, contemplating the raw material present in this moment. We can try to observe, reflect upon, and understand what is actually in front of us. We can be alert to the slight course correction, the specific need, and when it materializes, as we are able, we can act.

WAYFINDER EXERCISE

DETERMINE YOUR REALITY

1. **Reach out.** Focus your attention on a single detail in the space in which you sit. It might be an object, a person, an idea. What is it? Why has it drawn your attention? Sit in silence for a moment. Then ask yourself, *Might this detail reveal something deeper about me and my own spirituality? About what matters to me?*

2. **Set your intention.** While your particular focus can determine your reality, it should always be your

goal to uncover truth, to connect with the world and its inhabitants based on how things really are. How can a change in focus uncover something new and real about your world?

Make your mantra by completing this sentence: *Deeper focus reveals . . .* what? Repeat that mantra several times. Be mindful of your breath.

3. **Review the past.** As you repeat your mantra, allow your mind to wander. Where does it go? Are you thinking of a moment from earlier today, earlier this year, or many years ago? Where does your focus fall? What comes in and out of focus?

   Settle on a single moment. What insight does this moment reveal to you?

4. **Always in motion.** The moment you've settled on from your past necessarily informs your present and might guide you into the future. What about your passions, values, and concerns does this place of focus invite you to better understand?

5. **This is the way.** Informed by your reflection, commit to some small action you can take in the near future. What is it? What will it require? Will you need to alter your focus in daily living?

End your reflection by cultivating a disposition of gratitude to yourself, the universe, and the infinite Other.

CHAPTER 3

WOUNDS

"Battles leave scars," says Jedi-turned-rebel Kanan Jarrus in "The Last Battle," an episode in the third season of *Star Wars: Rebels.* "Some you can't see."[14]

Kanan is referring to the psychological trauma that Captain Rex, a veteran of the Clone Wars, carries with him each day. Rex's body is whole, but his mind and his soul are hurting. Things he's seen, things he's done, people he's lost, opportunities he didn't pursue—he's haunted. But Captain Rex refuses to let the past govern his future. Ultimately, the wounds he carries with him—scars left behind by countless battles, by disappointments and failures—make him the hero we meet in *Rebels.* This is a hero who, though imperfect and struggling, still stands by his friends. He is still committed to doing good in a galaxy that is under the oppressive thumb of the Empire.

Captain Rex has made a choice. He has chosen to fight for the Rebellion, yes. But Rex has also chosen to refuse to let his past failures and his current woundedness define him, limit him, paralyze him.

This is a choice we can make in our own spiritual lives, perhaps over and over again. So much of our spiritual journey is making sense of and showing compassion toward our invisible inner wounds, places of supposed weaknesses. It's not easy to embrace our wounded selves, to incorporate those hurts into our stories. It might require a change of focus, a widening of the lens. That will be the work of this chapter.

What makes those words spoken by Kanan Jarrus so significant—a recognition of inner woundedness and all it entails—is that Kanan had only just recently begun to come to terms with his *own* battle scars. What might we learn from him?

A PADAWAN NO MORE

The young Padawan Kanan Jarrus watched his Jedi Master, Depa Billaba, get gunned down at the end of the Clone Wars. His friends-turned-enemies, the clone troopers, had betrayed him and his fellow Jedi in the wake of Order 66, and Kanan rightly fled. The trauma, pain, and doubt he endured forced him to find a new life well beyond the boundaries of the fallen Jedi, their temples, and their practices. He worked as a freight pilot and spent long hours at the cantina.[15] No longer part of a community serving a larger purpose, he looked out only for himself.

"Kanan is a Jedi that has very much . . . given up being a Jedi," reflects Dave Filoni, executive producer and executive creative director at Lucasfilm.[16] Nonetheless, Kanan finds himself begrudgingly swept up in the burgeoning Rebel Alliance. He becomes the reluctant master to Force-sensitive Ezra Bridger. Even so, and though this demonstrates progress, he's not yet ready to give himself fully to a cause larger than the needs of his own immediate crew.

At the conclusion of *Rebels*' second season, Kanan, Ezra, and former Jedi Ahsoka Tano travel to the planet Malachor. It's a place all Jedi are told to avoid. But they've been sent by Yoda to chase down the knowledge he thinks they need so that Darth Vader's Inquisitors (Force-sensitive, red lightsaber-wielding hunters who have been causing trouble for Jedi survivors and their rebel allies alike) can be destroyed. On Malachor, our heroes encounter an array of adversaries, including Maul, the not-at-all-dead villain of *The Phantom Menace*. The former Sith Lord aids in the defeat of Vader's Inquisitors and then turns his double-sided, bloodred blade on Kanan, slicing his face and blinding him. The older Jedi goes down. Maul, thinking Kanan easy prey, moves in to finish him off. But Kanan gets back up, reignites his blue blade, and, capitalizing on Maul's overconfidence, sends the Sith warrior toppling over a ledge. (True to form, Maul is not dead yet.)

Kanan, now sightless, once again reverts to questioning his worth, purpose, and decisions.

At the time of the episode's release, Dave Filoni was quick to bat down any thought that Kanan's wound was insignificant. "People think, 'Oh, but the Force will allow him to do things.' The Force is not a superpower. It doesn't work that way. It's a matter of what you're willing to believe. I think the story that we tell with Kanan and his blindness is simple—you are as limited as you allow yourself to be."[17]

You are as limited as you allow yourself to be—that's the key. It's about what you believe about yourself and your place in the galaxy. It's about what you choose to focus on.

CANNONBALL MOMENTS

In the Ignatian tradition, we talk about "cannonball moments."[18] The phrase refers to hinge experiences that have the potential to alter the trajectory of our lives. A cannonball moment is an event that's loaded with spiritual significance. It begs the question: How do we respond to moments of great import—moments that may be riddled with trauma, grief, agony, and despair?

Ignatius of Loyola was a soldier long before he lived the life of a mystic saint. It was his arrogance and pride, a desire to prove himself and his own worth, that led him to refuse to surrender when French forces surrounded his troops at the Battle of Pamplona. The year was 1521. The French fired on his position, and a cannonball struck Ignatius. One leg was shattered, the other grievously wounded. His days as a soldier were over. The injuries he sustained and the deaths of his companions were utterly unnecessary. Ignatius was faced with a choice of how he would respond to this moment. How would he write the next chapter of his story?

Because the first operation had left his legs uneven, and he couldn't bear the thought of returning to courtly life with an unsightly limp, Ignatius insisted that his doctors rebreak and reset the broken bones. But no matter how many times the doctors tore at his legs, their efforts would not heal his pride. He lay in his bed dreaming of the glamorous lifestyle to which he would never return.

This is the kind of life-altering trauma that shapes saint and Jedi alike. A cannonball blows up not only your dreams but also the way you see yourself in the past, present, and any potential future. It's likely you, too, have a moment (or several) in mind where your entire world hinged on decisions made in response to a seismic event. It's challenging to expand the imagination beyond what we know, to dream up a world and a future that not only survive the injury at hand but also transcend it. We're faced with the task of incorporating into the person we will become that which left us scarred. This spiritual work isn't easy.

Pitfalls abound. It's tempting—and sometimes seemingly simpler—to assume this new wound is all you will ever be. Systemic family therapist Richard C. Schwartz writes of this temptation in his book *No Bad Parts*: "You identify with your weakness, assuming that who you really are is defective and that if other people saw the real you, they'd be repulsed."[19] Maybe you lie in bed all day and think of yourself as a *former* soldier, a *former* Jedi. You are not able to move beyond your wound, treat yourself with compassion, and embrace the new opportunities at hand.

Talk about misplaced focus determining the wrong reality!

"No one can help anyone without becoming involved, without entering with his or her whole person into the painful situation, without taking the risk of becoming hurt, wounded, or even destroyed in the process," writes the eminent spiritual author and Dutch priest Henri Nouwen. "The great illusion of leadership is to think that others can be led out of the desert by someone who has never been there."[20]

It's not a matter of *if* we're wounded. In this life, that's inevitable. It's a matter of our response. The question, then, for this process of healing is: What—who—are we living for? And are we able to hold whatever—whomever—it is at the forefront of our mind as we make that long journey from woundedness to wholeness?

WE CARRY CONFLICT

Through contemplative prayer, Ignatius discovered that the God of the universe was inviting him to lay down his sword and pick up a pilgrim staff, to serve those in need, and to spread a message of mercy, love, and compassion. His pride was something he could learn from, and then share the resulting lessons with others.

Kanan Jarrus, too, engages in a bit of contemplation on the planet Atollon, the location of the new Rebel base. He discerns a mysterious voice calling to him from the wilderness. While his friends go on a mission, he sets out in search of the source of the voice, which he discovers to be a mystical Force creature called the Bendu.

"You carry conflict with you," the Bendu observes. Kanan assumes the creature is referring to the Sith holocron in his possession. Kanan himself had become nearly obsessed with the item, so worried was he over the influence it was having on Ezra. But the Bendu quickly refuses to let Kanan take the easy way out; it's not a mere object that is causing Kanan's hardship, powerful as that object may be. Kanan is carrying the conflict *within*. And he's refusing to look at it squarely.

The Bendu presses the Jedi Knight, insisting, "Only you can change yourself." The Bendu pushes Kanan to stop seeking out external excuses for his current state and instead look within.

Then it clicks: "Fear, grief, anger—that's how I see myself," Kanan realizes. What he sees clearly now is something he *does* have control over. He can change what he believes himself to be. He can change his focus.

"If you can see yourself, you never will be truly blind." With those words from the Bendu, Kanan sets off to help his friends. He *does* have a part to play in the wider galaxy. He *does* have something he would give his life for.

The Bendu's words resonate here, too, in this galaxy oh-so-near. Looking plainly at our woundedness, discovering the possibilities within, and embracing the totality of ourselves set us on a path of greater good. Upon that path, we encounter our greatest potential. How might our own flaws and shortcomings actually help us in becoming the best version of ourselves?

MAUL VERSUS KENOBI; REVENGE VERSUS REPAIR

This approach stands in contrast to the path of the dark side. "Revenge does wonders for the will to live," says the impaled but not-at-all-dead Grand Inquisitor in the penultimate episode of *Obi-Wan Kenobi*.

Think again of Maul. Here we see a character wounded and unable to transcend that wound. That devastating blow to his body and his ego at the conclusion of *The Phantom Menace* sets the trajectory for the rest of his story. He could not move past his desire for revenge against Obi-Wan Kenobi, the Jedi who defeated him. This burden he carried consumed him, clouded his focus, governed every action he took from his resurrection in *The Clone Wars* to his ultimate demise in *Rebels*. We learn that everything Maul says and does in relation to Kanan and Ezra is driving him toward a singular purpose: Discover Obi-Wan's hiding place, and destroy him. Unfortunately for Maul, when he does, Obi-Wan makes short work of him.

This unresolved wound breaks the former Sith Lord— and reminds us how essential it is to heal, repair, integrate, and move on after a cannonball moment.

We can walk the path of Maul or the path of Ignatius.

There's a wonderful line in the finale of *Obi-Wan Kenobi*. Darth Vader, facing his former master—and seemingly surprised at the fight old Ben is putting up—declares, "Your strength has returned, but the weakness still remains." Vader goes on to say this is why Kenobi is destined to lose. But the Dark Lord is wrong. Kenobi triumphs, using his strengths, weaknesses, and everything in between.

This is how we live our lives, isn't it? We never fully heal some wounds; we never fully overcome some weaknesses. But we see them. We come to know and understand them. Perhaps we welcome them, despite the hardship they represent. We show compassion to ourselves, and in so doing we emerge from our own deserts with the ability to help others journey out of theirs. Our focus widens; we see beyond weakness to the whole person. Wounds are not the end of the story. Often, they can be the start of an entirely new one.

WAYFINDER EXERCISE

BUT WEAKNESS REMAINS

1. **Reach out.** Sink into yourself. Examine the different parts of who you are. Wiggle your toes; blink your eyes. Do you feel any distress, tension, or woundedness in yourself? Does that part of you draw your attention outside of yourself in any way?

2. **Set your intention.** Consider how your inner sense of distress might be inviting you to make connections to something larger. Consider, too, how an inner or literal wound might be sucking up too much of your focus, thereby preventing you from bringing your full self to bear on some other issue in your world.

   Make your mantra by completing this sentence: *I am more than my woundedness. I am* . . . what? Repeat that mantra several times. Be mindful of your breath.

3. **Review the past.** As you repeat your mantra, allow your mind to wander. Where does it go? Are you thinking of a moment from earlier today, earlier this year, or from years ago? Are there unresolved wounds that require healing? Do you detect the source(s) of your distress? Are there patterns therein that are revelatory? How have you allowed yourself to be limited by past wounds? How have you transcended them?

   Settle on a single moment. What insight does this moment reveal to you?

4. **Always in motion.** The moment you've settled on from your past necessarily informs your present and might guide you into the future. How can you, whole yet wounded, bring your unique self into the next instant of need, whether for yourself or others?

5. **This is the way.** Informed by your reflection, commit to some small action you can take in the near future. What is it? What will it require? More healing? The gift of healing for others? How will you attain that?

End your reflection by cultivating a disposition of gratitude to yourself, the universe, and the infinite Other.

CHAPTER 4

STRUCTURES

When, in the wake of Yoda's death, the Force ghost of Obi-Wan Kenobi strides out of the shadowy swamp of Dagobah, Luke Skywalker is not happy to see him. Kenobi tries to placate his former student by assuring him that Yoda will still "be with him." But that's not what's on Luke's mind.

Kenobi lied about Vader, about Anakin, and about Luke's connection to the Dark Lord of the Sith. Well, at least from a certain point of view.

Now that Luke sees Vader as more than a monster, as a person trapped in a system of oppression and suffering, he can't help but rethink his whole plan and purpose. He can't kill his father! Obi-Wan shrugs off Luke's anger. It seems that Kenobi gave up on Anakin Skywalker years ago, unable to save him from Vader. But Luke insists there's still good to be found in Anakin.

"He's more machine now than man," Kenobi counters. "Twisted and evil."

Old Ben's retort is easily dismissed. He's simply describing what he sees. Vader is *literally* a man trapped in a machine, without which he'd certainly die. But something else keeps him going, too. Rage. If we pause for a moment and reflect on Kenobi's words, we glimpse the spiritual stakes: More machine than human. Twisted and evil. What does Obi-Wan *really* mean? And what might his words convey to us?

In this chapter, we turn to the oppressive systems and structures that intersect our spiritual lives, often without our even realizing it, and we ask what we can do to unravel and resist them.

Perhaps, like Luke, we'll catch a glimpse of ourselves behind Vader's mask.

DID WE KILL ANAKIN SKYWALKER?

Let's return to Obi-Wan's retort: More machine than man. Kenobi isn't *really* bemoaning Vader's prosthetics or his reliance on technology to help him breathe. He's lamenting that his old friend has become so caught up in the enterprise of evil that he can no longer see a way out. He can no longer imagine another path for himself. He's given up on what once was, as well as on the hope of what might yet be.

We don't need to understand the mechanics behind Darth Vader's suit to appreciate Kenobi's meaning. The man who once was Anakin Skywalker is now so caught up in the machinery of the dark side that he is more a tool of evil than a human being fully alive and free to exercise his conscience.

Thinking back to our previous chapter, Anakin's wound, by Kenobi's reckoning and Vader's own actions, appears too great to heal. Luke would prove them both wrong, but their pessimism is understandable.

Remember that haunting moment in the *Obi-Wan Kenobi* finale? In the aftermath of their duel, Vader—his mask shattered, the sunken, pale face of the man who once was Anakin Skywalker glaring at his old master—stammers, "You didn't kill Anakin Skywalker. I did."

Vader, and the machinery of evil that he manifests, killed the legendary Jedi.

From the vantage point of this solitary episode—and certainly from Luke's point of view in the swamp of Dagobah—this claim seems like a clever bit of narrative work. Arguably, that's exactly what it was. Even so, the truth of the claim—this idea that the very structures of evil present in the galaxy can twist and pervert a person so thoroughly as to rob them of their humanity, perhaps without their even realizing it—is one worth pondering.

And is Obi-Wan *really* off the hook? The dark side was at work all around him for years, but he failed to see it. Like nearly every other Jedi, he failed to act. In truth, he *contributed* to the dark side's cause, most notably in his role as general during the Clone Wars. That was all part of Darth Sidious's master plan. Kenobi may not have been the one to deliver the killing blow to Anakin, but his blindness to the truth of what was happening all around him certainly didn't help his old Padawan. Kenobi doesn't bear full responsibility for Anakin's fall, but neither is he blameless.

Do we recognize the machinery of our own society that keeps us trapped in cycles of evil? The machinery that sustains structures of injustice, violence, and oppression? Do we see clearly those habits we unthinkingly perpetuate? And are we able to understand the impact that our own shameful tendencies has on ourselves as well as on our community and the world?

Luke believed that there was not only some good left in his father but that there was also a way in which the good might yet lead him to reclaim his life. But it all depended on

Vader recognizing the evil systems and impulses in which he was entangled, and having the courage to throw the manifestation of that evil down a reactor shaft.[21]

AWAKENING TO INJUSTICE

In the First Week of his Spiritual Exercises, Ignatius of Loyola invites us to look plainly at sin and its effects in our life and our world. This exercise is not meant to be a guilt trip but rather to awaken in us an understanding of the spiritual stakes, the evil that is at work in sinister, unnoticed ways throughout society. If we don't take an honest, hard look at sin—structural and otherwise—and our culpability in it, we can never discover true spiritual freedom. In short, we're challenged to wake up to reality.

"To really understand evil, Ignatius has us ask for interior knowledge, a 'feel' for how the world works and deep repugnance for its disorder," writes Fr. Dean Brackley, SJ in *The Call to Discernment in Troubled Times*. "We want clear-sighted realism about people and institutions . . . and ourselves. We want to be able to sniff out the evil lurking behind warm smiles, political platforms, pious rhetoric, and advertising."[22]

We might think of this as complementary to living as a contemplative in action: we don't simply *promote* love; we also work to ferret out its opposite wherever it is found, even if it's found within our very selves.

Brackley's description of evil hiding behind a warm smile brings to mind Chancellor Palpatine, that seemingly harmless old leader of the Galactic Republic. His smile, his politics, his rhetoric—all these things masked his true self.

That true self was a Sith Lord manipulating the downfall of the Republic, the Jedi, and a society that was striving for justice and peace.

Palpatine's early interest in and manipulation and perversion of Anakin Skywalker illustrates the machinery of larger systems and structures at play over the Jedi's fate. Anakin is responsible for his decisions, yes. At the same time, forces were in motion around him that he didn't detect, didn't know existed, let alone know how to fight against. Not only was the dark side literally flourishing under Anakin's nose, but the entire enterprise known as the Clone Wars was an orchestrated plot to undermine the democratic order it sought to uphold. In all his ignorance, Anakin's willing participation in the Clone Wars helped normalize the concept that the supposed peacekeepers of the galaxy should lead soldiers into battle.

We begin to see how an uncritical approach to the systems, structures, and common wisdom that uphold society can lead us to participate in the machinations of evil. Personal failure and societal failure: both can contribute to mistakes, disorder, and chaos. Evil is more than happy to take advantage of any available tool.

HOW DO YOU MEASURE A WEEK?

Everyone who makes the Spiritual Exercises of St. Ignatius of Loyola passes through four "weeks." Ignatius uses the word *week* loosely; it's better to think of this measurement of time as a spiritual *movement*.[23] And the first movement is all about sinking into the problems of our world.

Let me give an example from my experience of the Exercises. During my retreat, when I contemplated the First Week a clear image came to mind of Baltimore, Maryland, where I lived. I saw individuals who struggled to find permanent housing. They were forced to live on the streets and in shelters, wrestle with extreme temperatures, mental health issues, and the constant search for food and resources. This is a macro problem, and it's easy to shake our fists in anger at such injustice!

But my contemplation of the First Week, which is to say my meditation on this particular social problem, did not stop at the macro. As my prayer continued, I saw the faces and figures of unhoused women and men that I walk or drive past day after day. I grappled with my reactions to such experiences, which included frustration, fear, disgust, and disdain. I came face-to-face with my own responsibility, my own biases and shortcomings, my own role in upholding this injustice, my own inability to offer even small solutions. Sure, I've been known to give money now and again, to buy folks in need a sandwich, but even more frequently I look the other way, ignoring the problem and its many faces. As my reflection went on, it became clear that this wasn't simply a macro problem for others to work out; I had a role to play and indeed had played a role in it, too.

Contemplating the First Week is an exercise in examining the interconnected web of injustice and human error that entangles and chokes our world. We begin to see past the macro and dig into the specific. It feels uncomfortable to address our own complicity and inevitable culpability in perpetuating injustice. Yet, this is an important spiritual task, a necessary step in building up the reality we want to live in. We adjust our focus. We heal our wounds and those of others. By examining the role we play—good and bad—in our communities, we cultivate within ourselves the disposition we need to throw off the status quo. Our new understanding breeds new opportunities for action.

There are countless other examples of how we can sink into the problems of the world. Climate change is a macro problem that is devastating our world; our own micro contribution is the number of plastic water bottles we buy. Loneliness is a spiritual ill that plagues everyone from time to time; when we avoid others, or neglect paying a visit to our grandparents, or refuse to smile at that person on the other side of the subway car, we may be perpetuating the loneliness status quo. Racism, sexism, misogyny, homophobia, and Islamophobia are some of the macro systems that maintain and reinforce injustice. Our spiritual lives demand that we not only point out these travesties but also do the hard work of recognizing the role we play in their perpetuation. We must get better at seeing how these systems are affecting our lives and the decisions we make.

Does this sound like a hopeless enterprise? It can seem that way if we allow ourselves to sink into fear and despair. If we do nothing *but* point at injustice and our own personal failures, we spiral. We get stuck. In that way, the evil to which the First Week is meant to awaken us consumes us instead.

There's a reason this is the *First* Week. Understanding evil's presence in our world is a starting point, not an ending. The Christian message—and, by extension, Ignatian spirituality—is all about being liberated from darkness and failure and shame so that we are free to imagine a future built upon hope, compassion, justice, and peace.

But we can't be liberated if we don't realize we're imprisoned. Meanwhile, the evil we don't fully see can and does manipulate us from the shadows.

FEAR AND FAILURE

It's obvious to any casual viewer of Star Wars that Anakin Skywalker was manipulated by the dark side before he embraced it. He didn't begin as the saga's villain; he began as the hero. He wanted to do good. And, coming out of his troubled childhood on Tatooine—responding to those tiny grains of sand—he had very explicit desires. He wanted to free others who had been enslaved as he had been. He wanted to free his mother. And he wanted to build a better galaxy.

Those desires, coupled with his natural talent as a Force wielder (So. Many. Midi-chlorians!) positioned Anakin for success. He knew well the evil the galaxy was capable of, and now he knew he had the wherewithal to confront that evil head-on. What he lacked was the ability to process his own shortcomings, to recognize that even he, the "Chosen One," was neither perfect nor all-powerful.

Anakin's lack of both ultimate power and self-awareness are encapsulated in his failure to save his mother, Shmi, from the Tusken Raiders who abducted her. Crying, sorrowful, and ashamed, he realizes he's not strong enough to save her. In that moment, he promises himself and the memory of his mother that he *will become* strong enough and he *will not* fail again. Rather than accept this failure, Anakin refuses to see himself as not all-powerful. He hunts the Tuskens and slaughters them. It's a bad decision. Obviously, rather than focus on healing his wound, he shoves it aside as he renders another.

This is a solitary if horrific incident, and Anakin is rightly shocked by his own actions. But it's not long before this struggling Jedi—grief-stricken by the loss of his mother and reeling from the violence he's perpetrated against an entire community—is put in charge of a battalion of clone troopers and told to go to war. Anakin is a great warrior; again and again he is commended for his success on the battlefield, despite its unorthodoxy. He trains his own Padawan, Ahsoka Tano, to follow in his footsteps, and together they amass more and more victories as they come to the aid of those caught in the path of war and conquest. Justice and peace—enforced via lightsaber.

And so, when Anakin is haunted by nightmares of the death of his wife, Padmé Amidala, in childbirth, he seeks a way to change his fate. He assumes there is something he—and he alone—can *do*, some enemy he can *defeat*. He is powerful; with more power, he must be able to emerge victorious, even over death. Desperate to find that power, fear has him trapped.

Enter Chancellor Palpatine—or rather, Darth Sidious. The Sith Lord orchestrated the war. He ensured that Anakin was praised for his valiancy in battle. He has even encouraged the Jedi to seek out more accolades, of which he is certainly deserving. And then he lets slip that, yes, in fact there *is* a way to cheat death. You just have to embrace the dark side of the Force.

Anakin has come this far. He can't allow himself to be defeated. He can't fail again to protect those who are most important to him. He's become so entangled within Palpatine's web—the shadowy system of power being built by the future emperor—that Anakin is now actually serving the interests of Sidious.

That's why he so quickly kills Mace Windu. That's why when Sidious bellows, "DO WHAT MUST BE DONE!" Anakin doesn't ask what he means. The system must be maintained. Resistance must be eliminated, no matter what form it takes. Skywalker-turned-Vader will do what he must to avoid failure, to protect what he holds to be most important. His once-noble desire to free others from tyranny has been twisted into that fateful line uttered on Mustafar: "If you're not with me, then you're my enemy."

Anakin, in his desire to ensure and maintain his own self-worth and grip on power, aligns himself completely with the burgeoning interests of the Empire even as he fails to see how his personal decisions are undermining all he once stood for. Instead, he gives up his personal agency to the whims of the Emperor.

HUMILITY UNRAVELS DARKNESS

As troubling as it may be, we can all see something of ourselves in the fall of Anakin Skywalker. We all run the risk of upholding or creating structures of injustice if we fail to look at our personal decisions and communal responsibilities. We perpetuate the system to protect our own interests, afraid that if we don't, what we hold dear will be taken from us.

We cannot allow fear to govern our choices.

When the newly minted Darth Vader storms into the Jedi Temple and slaughters the younglings, we're shocked. Obi-Wan is nearly brought to tears. And yet, isn't this the logical extension of evil? Isn't this just violence doing what violence is destined to do? It's shocking only if we haven't been paying attention. What do we think Anakin and his troopers were doing on all those Separatist planets throughout the Clone Wars?

Let's reflect again on systems in our own galaxy. An easy example is capitalism and its pervasive, often unseen influence on our lives. It's easy to shrug off an economic system as just the way things are. We human beings are more than our economics, right? The way we buy and sell goods doesn't dictate how we live our actual lives.

Dean Brackley, SJ, disagrees. "Capitalism aggravates the universal desire to possess and rewards covetousness."[24] Does this claim ring true in our lives? Do we look closely at what this system does to others? We like to imagine ourselves as generous, mindful of the needs of those around us. But something insidious is going on in the background. Brackley goes on to say, "As paths for social climbing narrow and upward mobility turns into a more ruthless game of hardball, we are awakening to the disquieting fact that it is impossible for everyone, or even the majority, to enjoy the affluent lifestyle of the world's middle classes."[25]

In other words, there are necessarily losers in this system that relies on fueling infinite wants amid finite resources, particularly as we take a global perspective. We want to hold fast to what we have; we want to reach for more while we still can. We want to be winners. Losing means suffering, sorrow, death—and children are not spared. Are we in fact also holding that lightsaber in the Jedi Temple? Not directly, no. But we're part of the system.

So how do we flip the script? How do we get out from under these oppressive structures? That's the work of the First Week of the Spiritual Exercises. Ignatius must have known it wasn't easy because he devoted one-fourth of his entire spiritual system to this project.

To start, as Brackley explains, "Ignatius assigns humil-ity a central role in our lives. For only in its soil can love take root, grow and bear fruit. To be authentic, however, humil-ity must be solidarity."[26] Ignatius is pointing to a radically countercultural way of proceeding. The path of humility was foundational for Ignatius. "Humility flowers into soli-darity, identifying with others to the point of sharing their suffering."[27] That means we give up some of our security. We put ourselves at risk.

Isn't that what Luke Skywalker did on the second Death Star? He surrendered himself and was taken before the mani-festation of all that was evil in the galaxy. And when con-fronted by the Emperor, he eventually threw aside his weapon, embracing the path of nonviolence. To be sure, he suffered for it, as Palpatine's Force lightening pulsed through his bones.

But this act of nonviolence, of surrender, of accept-ing failure and defeat, was the antidote to the machinations of evil that had ensnared Anakin Skywalker. Luke resisted the easy path. He could have accepted Palpatine's offer and become his newest apprentice. But where Anakin did as Palpatine instructed, clinging to whatever assurances he could that what he loved would not be lost, Luke resisted that temptation. He knew there was nothing more he could do to help his friends on the forest moon of Endor. Humbly, he accepted his fate, placing his life in the hands of others. Luke's courage and sacrifice broke through to his father, and Vader cast Palpatine down that reactor shaft.

The system relied upon violence, selfishness, shame, and secrecy. Luke's actions illuminated the lie of those vices, and the system began to crumble as a result.

As we progress in our own spiritual journeys, what do we need to throw down the reactor shaft of our lives?

MORE MACHINE THAN HUMAN

1. **Reach out.** Imagine your community, the place in which you live and call home. In your mind, reach out to the many people who live here, and the creatures, the animals, and plants. What do you sense of their lives and experience? Is something holding them back? Is something holding *you* back from a full and flourishing life?

2. **Set your intention.** Consider how invisible forces at work in your society may be stifling the progress of entire communities. Have you been blind to these hidden forces? Have you perpetuated them? Are you, yourself, held back from achieving your greatest potential as a result of them? Commit to unraveling this web of lies.

   Make your mantra by completing this sentence: *I open my eyes to see* . . . what? Repeat that mantra several times. Be mindful of your breath.

3. **Review the past.** As you repeat your mantra, allow your mind to wander. Where does it go? Are you thinking of a moment from earlier today, earlier this year, or many years ago? Is there an instance—or perhaps many—when some invisible force worked against the greater good in your community? How did you respond? Did you summon an equal or

greater force—perhaps an act of nonviolence to counter a system built on violence?

Settle on a single moment. What insight does this moment reveal to you?

4. **Always in motion.** The moment you've settled on from your past necessarily informs your present and might guide you into the future. What small act of resistance can you take to counter the prevailing system of injustice you've identified in your reflection? How might that action change life for yourself and others?

5. **This is the way.** Imagine the future that might unfold when hidden systems of oppression are unraveled and all of humanity is able to flourish.

End your reflection by cultivating a disposition of gratitude to yourself, the universe, and the infinite Other.

PART 1 REPRISE

EMBRACE THE AWAKENING

The first part of this book has been about identifying phantom menaces, both good and bad, that pester and prod us. These spiritual nudges can help us imagine a world and a purpose bigger than ourselves, bigger than we'd previously dared dream. We find ourselves stumbling into adventure. But these spiritual menaces can also hamper our journey, limit our horizons, and cause us to spiral if we don't recognize them for what they are.

In short, the first part of this book was about awakening to the forces around us.

"There has been an awakening," Supreme Leader Snoke says. "Have you felt it?" Kylo Ren replies that he has. The awakening, as Snoke notes and we the viewers come to see, isn't in itself a good or bad thing. It encompasses both the light *and* the dark. In the sequel trilogy, this awakening points to the resurgences of both the Jedi *and* the Sith.

So, too, in our own spiritual awakening. We look at our desires. We examine the values we hold closely. We recognize our own inevitable woundedness and the various systems within society that continue to do us and our neighbors harm. We awaken to these realities and, in so doing, we have the opportunity to go deeper and seize this depth of knowledge to better understand who we really are and what we really mean to the world at large.

"Your True Self is who you objectively are from the moment of your creation," writes the Franciscan mystic, Richard Rohr.[28] This is the goal of the spiritual life, of any spiritual journey: to enter more deeply into who we *actually* are, and to find peace there. In that finding is born a desire to bring others to this deeper understanding. Therein we see the importance of community and the necessary overflowing into justice, compassion, sustainability, and mercy.

We also glimpse the role of religion itself. "The only and single purpose of religion is to lead you to a regular experience of this True Self," Rohr claims.[29] This necessarily takes place within community. We know ourselves more and more completely within relationships. With others. With the divine. Capital *M* Mystery meeting mystery, without and within.

We wake up to this call, to this spiritual invitation and the work it requires. And it *is* work. As Fr. Rohr says, "Practice is important because mere willpower ('I will do it!') or enforced behavior ('You must go to church on Sunday!') does not actually change our attitude or interior space."[30]

When we find ourselves trapped in darkness or self-pity, it's tempting to cast about in every direction for an exit route. We make impulsive, often ill-advised decisions. Instead, let's open our eyes to see clearly who we are and what we're about. Darkness is inevitable; we have all experienced moments of such challenge before, and we inevitably will do so again. But the answer is not to stick our heads in the sand or take the first escape pod out into the great unknown. The answer lies within. Who are we? Who are we invited to become? How can we intentionally take steps to get there?

Sand. Focus. Wounds. Structures. Deep desires. Personal values. Contemplation and action. Cannonball moments. Looking at injustice with a clear-eyed focus.

Spend time with these concepts. You might find they'll help you become more powerful—spiritually speaking, that is—than you've ever imagined.

PART 2

ENGAGING THE DUEL OF THE FATES

One of the most epic lightsaber duels in the whole Star Wars franchise takes place behind closed doors: Qui-Gon Jinn and Obi-Wan Kenobi versus the newly rediscovered Sith Lord Darth Maul. Cue the music.

The stakes are high, not just for our heroes but for the whole galaxy. The Sith are back! They've been pulling the strings all along! They've infiltrated . . . well, that's still to be discovered. Where are they? What is their plan? The only thing the Jedi know for the moment is that this spiky-headed Zabrak warrior must be defeated. The return of the Sith would be devastating to the peace and prosperity of the galaxy, and the Jedi can't allow that to happen.

We see the battle play out on the big screen. Shots of whirling laser swords are interspersed between scenes of the Theed Royal Guard (led by Padmé Amidala and Captain Panaka), the Gungan army, and a contingent of Naboo N-1 starfighters pushing back the invading Trade Federation forces. We viewers know that the battle for this singular planet's future is caught up in the future of the galaxy writ large. We discover that although the sinister Sith plot includes the events unfolding on Naboo, Naboo is just one piece in an enormous and intricate puzzle.

And yet, when Obi-Wan and Qui-Gon separate from the forces of Padmé and Panaka and take off to engage Maul in the hangar bay of the palace, the blast doors slam shut behind them. This all-important duel between Jedi and Sith, the light and the dark, two distinct and disparate views for the galaxy, takes place out of sight of the Naboo and Gungan soldiers on the front lines. Naboo and Gungan alike are fighting the good fight without realizing the dueling fates on the other side of that door. The people of Naboo *know* the stakes are high. And yet, they didn't, or couldn't, see just how high, nor could they see how interconnected their efforts were in the fate of the galaxy.

This happens in our spiritual life, too. Perhaps not on such an epic scale. But how many of us have become obsessed (and rightly so) with our own *stuff*—our struggles, challenges, and responsibilities—that we fail to see the larger picture? We don't see the spiritual stakes. We fail to recognize just how interconnected our lives are with those of others who are near, far, and in between.

Sometimes, it's easier to hunker down and zero in on what *we* need to accomplish. And with our attention directed inward, we fail to hear the *buzz hiss* of the lightsaber duel taking place on the other side of the proverbial door.

We fail, I think, to account for that duel of the fates—the spirits of good and less-than good whirling about in our day-to-day.

In the first section of this book, we awoke to the spiritual life pulsing around us, and to the phantom menaces we encounter in our lives. We trained our eyes inward on ourselves and outward on our world so that we could see all things brimming with the spark of mystery. We recognized that we each have a role to play, and we took steps to discover just what that role might be. We pondered the impact that external systems and structures have on us, without our even realizing it.

In part 2, we will begin to discern those hidden forces at work on us, and identify the effect they have on our lives. In the Ignatian tradition, we can identify these "forces" as warring spirits, good and bad. Which spirits help us become who we are meant to be? Which spirits distract and push us off course? We have to examine these spiritual forces closely so as to make good decisions.

How will we do this? Ignatius of Loyola discovered various rules for discerning these spirits. But those rules, hard won, were discovered in his own version of the Dark Side Cave as he wrestled with spirits good and less so. We begin there, in the cave with Ignatius and Luke Skywalker, so that we can map out our own caves. We then deepen our engagement with these wayward spirits and discover Ignatius's rules reflected in Force visions and special editions alike. The final chapter in this section will explore one of Ignatius's most important meditations, the "Two Standards," which helps us place our lives on a trajectory that ultimately leads toward the light, even as it helps us stay ever mindful of the constant pull of the dark.

Simply waking up to the spiritual life isn't enough; we need to discover what it's about, discern how our own spiritual path is blazed. A young Luke Skywalker, while training on Dagobah, asks Yoda if the dark side of the Force is stronger than the light. Yoda says no, that it's only easier and more seductive. And that might be true. But we also know that, left to grow in the shadows, forgotten and ignored, the dark side becomes quite strong indeed, no matter how many Jedi insist that the Sith can't rise again. It's not wise to ignore the duel of the fates happening just down the hallway of our inner lives. We must engage in it.

From the Dark Side Cave of Dagobah to the ruins of Maz Kanata's castle, from Rey's fear to Ben Kenobi's shame and Kylo Ren's inability to let the past die, the second part of this book will be about our attempt to wrestle with Luke's question: *Is the dark side stronger?* And what is our response to its constant tug?

CHAPTER 5

CAVES

L et's head back to Dagobah for some more Jedi train-ing. I've always been fascinated by the Dark Side Cave. It's spiritually consequential. Luke realizes as much just by standing in front of it. He *knows* something's not quite right; he feels *cold*. Yoda confirms his suspicions. Indeed, the place is strong with the dark side.

All the same, Yoda insists that Luke enter the cave. Understandably, Luke wants to know what he'll find within.

"Only what you take with you," Yoda replies.

That's the line that gives me chills. What does he mean? What is Luke carrying? We quickly find out. Luke encounters a vision of Darth Vader—what we assume to be his great-est fear—and defeats it. He strikes Vader down, cuts off his head. But it's not the face of a monster Luke discovers behind the mask; it's his own. We begin to understand what Luke *really* fears, and that it was this fear that he brought with him into the cave.

In the wonderful collection of essays gathered in *Star Wars and Philosophy*, philosopher Judith Barad writes in her contribution, "The Aspiring Jedi's Handbook of Virtue,"

"[Luke] realizes that he's afraid of becoming evil, fears that his weakness of unrestrained anger and impatience would prevent him from becoming the Jedi he yearns to be. These fears are based on his failure to fully trust himself to resist temptation."[31]

Luke is afraid he'll fail and, in that moment of short-coming, become the very thing he swore to resist.

Is Luke surprised to encounter such a potential for darkness within himself? Perhaps. That's the mystery of the cave: Luke discovers something unknown within and without. A shadow of his own life, but also a bridge of empathy to another. In that cave, Luke discovers the hard truth that what befell Vader could just as easily befall him. The same temptations—the same systems and structures—still exist to pull him into darkness. How will Luke respond?

The Dark Side Cave isn't exclusive to Dagobah. We all must travel that cold, dark path into our own inner caves. What do *we* take with us? What do we discover about ourselves and our own lives, interwoven as they are in the lives of others? These are the questions to be faced in this chapter.

SAINTS IN A CAVE

Ignatius of Loyola also found himself in a cave.

While recovering from his battle wound at his family home in Loyola, Spain, Ignatius experienced a spiritual awakening. Fueled by his own contemplation of popular religious texts and a growing dissatisfaction with his old ways of living, Ignatius found his life infused with new meaning and purpose. Committing his life to God, he gave up his courtly life and took up the mantle of pilgrim.

Ignatius embraced his pilgrimage with vigor. He set out on foot, traversing the Basque countryside, visiting shrines and holy places. He laid his sword, the symbol of his old life, at the feet of Our Lady of Montserrat.

Eventually, however, doubt crept in.

Ignatius took shelter under a rocky outcropping near the Spanish town of Manresa, not far from the mountain-bound monastery of Montserrat. This "cave" holds a fascinating place in the Ignatian tradition. It is here that Ignatius drafted the *Spiritual Exercises*, which is the foundational text of all of Ignatian spirituality.

But in that same cave, as he wrote in the *Spiritual Exercises*, Ignatius struggled with shame, doubt, and fear of failure, to the point of suicidal ideation (a note to readers: Ignatius wrote in the third person). "The temptation often came over him with great force to throw himself through a large hole in his room, next to the place where he was praying."[32]

The thing that makes a cave a cave—whether in the mountains of Spain or the swamps of Dagobah—is the condition of darkness. And yet it is here where the absence of light is most striking that we begin to see things about ourselves that frighten us and make us weep. We see sides of ourselves we didn't think—or didn't want to believe—existed. But the darkness of those caves wins only if we fail to shine a bit of light.

We are much more than what we carry into the dark.

PLATO'S CAVE

In Plato's famous Allegory of the Cave, prisoners who are chained in darkness are unable to see one another. Their world consists only of shadowy figures cast by a blazing fire upon the cave's wall.

Despite this limited view of reality, the cave dwellers are content in what they think they know. In fact, they dwell in ignorance. They do not know what the world contains beyond those shadowy figures, let alone what they themselves might contribute. Worse, they don't care to know.

When one of the prisoners is released, stands up, looks around, and realizes they've been duped, it's not relief that floods the mind but panic. The former prisoner now has a better understanding of the nature of reality. But the brightness of the blazing fire hurts the eyes, representing the pain that new knowledge—a paradigm shift resulting from a cannonball moment—can cause. That person, notes Barad, "may then have to change former beliefs, values and ways of doing things."[33]

Plato's allegory invites us to reflect on our own ignorance, our response to those who would free us from that ignorance, and our subsequent responsibility to free others. But our ignorance is not limited to those things we do not yet know about our world; it includes those things we do not yet know about ourselves. Our potential. Our beauty. Our power.

Will we let light shine in those dark places of our stories? Will we do what must be done to live in the light?

WHAT WE RISE ABOVE

One of my favorite lines in *Star Wars: Rebels* comes from an older, wiser, Tatooine-bound Obi-Wan Kenobi: "Look what I have risen above."[34]

He says this in response to the scornful words of Maul, the vengeful former Sith Lord who a younger Obi-Wan didn't quite manage to kill. Maul dismisses Kenobi as a rat lost in the desert.

The exchange is dramatic, and the ensuing fight is decisive. Obi-Wan does not get drawn into a flashy exchange of humming lightsabers. He defends himself from Maul's onslaught and quickly defeats his old foe, though not before making it clear that this is a fight he would rather have avoided.

Quite a change from the Obi-Wan we saw during the Clone Wars. In *Revenge of the Sith*, he leaps into a hangar full of battle droids, bent on chasing down the cyborg General Grievous with nothing but his lightsaber and a cheeky, "Hello, there!"

Those many years in the sand and sun of Tatooine have done more than age Kenobi. What *has* he risen above?

At the outset of Kenobi's TV show, *Obi-Wan Kenobi*, which is set several years prior to *Star Wars: Rebels*, we see Ben living as a hermit in a cave. Teeka, the Jawa trader, appears to be Kenobi's only regular visitor, and even he finds Ben's squalor unsettling. It's clear that Obi-Wan is a broken man, riddled by grief. His struggles parallel Ignatius's time in the cave outside Manresa.

This comes as no surprise. Obi-Wan did single-handedly train the man who would become Darth Vader, who would overthrow the Jedi, slaughter his friends, and play a pivotal role in the ascension of the oppressive Galactic Empire. Obi-Wan missed the signs. Others paid the price.

But until we revisited Obi-Wan in that self-titled series, some ten years after *Revenge of the Sith*, we hadn't seen him deal with the repercussions of either his actions or his inaction. From swashbuckling general to the desert recluse we meet in *A New Hope*, Kenobi's character appeared consistent in his confidence, his calm, his commitment to the Force. How could that be? Didn't he undergo some inner turmoil after leaving his best friend for dead? After watching all he'd fought for crumble and burn?

As it turns out, yes. Yes, he did.

In fact, when we meet Ben at the beginning of his self-titled series, he's the opposite of confident, calm, and committed. He has buried his lightsaber in the desert, broken his connection with the Force, and refused to help those in need—from a doomed fellow Jedi to Princess Leia Organa herself.

Obi-Wan's world is shattered all over again when he learns that Vader is far less dead than he had believed. That's his hard truth, his moment of either standing up in Plato's allegorical cave or shrinking back down, content to watch shadows dance on cavern walls.

At first, Kenobi is unable to handle the truth. We see as much in the first confrontation between the former master and apprentice: Vader utterly destroys the weakened, distracted Kenobi. Obi-Wan is whisked away to heal in body and soul.

And heal he does. Slowly, by trusting strangers, by making himself available to the needs of the galaxy, by allowing himself to again care for others—the young Leia, the imperial-turned-rebel Tala Durith, and even his fallen apprentice, Anakin—Kenobi finds himself once again strong with the Force.

So what has Kenobi really risen above? What's he referring to when he claims as much in his retort to Maul beneath the night sky of Tatooine? It's not that he can survive in an unforgiving desert or go on the occasional adventure. It's not even that he can reconnect with the Force or best his former friend in a duel.

Obi-Wan has risen above his grief and shame. Nothing demonstrates that quite as powerfully as when he abandons the Tatooine cave. We already know the kinds of thoughts that drive a man to call such an unforgiving place home: unworthiness, doubt, a lack of self-love, and acceptance.

But something changes within him. His past failures remain the same, yet he is no longer governed by them. He no longer obsesses over fixing them, atoning for them. Even in that final moment when Darth Vader's life was his to take—the apparent righting of Kenobi's great wrong—Ben walks away.

He is no longer going to simply survive; he is going to *live*. Obi-Wan is no longer trapped by a past that cannot change (more on that in chapter 7). Rather, he looks to the future, which is full of possibilities, including redemption, hope, and learning, and makes himself available to the needs therein.

It's not until after Obi-Wan rises above his shame, guilt, and self-doubt that he is able to see and speak with the Force ghost of his old master, Qui-Gon Jinn. Obi-Wan thinks that Qui-Gon has chosen to appear only now. But the old Jedi assures Obi-Wan that he had been there all along. "You just were not ready to see," he says.

What spiritual truths are we unable to see while we remain trapped in our caves? What new possibilities will we recognize when we set aside our own doubt and fear? What will we discover about ourselves that has been there all along?

CUT YOUR HAIR—AND LEAVE YOUR CAVE

Think again of Ignatius's time in the cave. It seems almost a cruel fact of the spiritual life that one place can contain both light and dark, the heights and the depths of our vocation.

We both glimpse the ultimate meaning of our lives and at the same time are paralyzed by our potential failings.

I visited Ignatius's cave in Manresa. The cave is now a chapel nestled within a Jesuit retreat and spirituality center. The cave is small and narrow. The cool stone wall presses up against you as you jockey to claim one of the few places to sit. It's peaceful.

My fellow pilgrims and I attended Mass inside that cave. Fr. Kevin Burke, SJ, one of our pilgrimage leaders, presided. He drew our attention to the interior struggles with which Ignatius wrestled in that very space. He noted how Ignatius famously stopped attending to his own personal needs, letting his hair and fingernails grow long. Ignatius took on the appearance that matched how he *assumed* God saw him: dirty, shameful, and one step away from failure.

What had Ignatius brought into that cave? Doubts. Fears. Uncertainties.

And what did Fr. Burke say to those of us gathered there? "The most important thing Ignatius did for God in this cave was cut his fingernails and trim his hair." Not writing the *Spiritual Exercises*. Not planting the seeds of the eventual Jesuit order. The greatest, most important thing that Ignatius did in this place was cut his nails and trim his hair. Because in so doing, Ignatius came back to himself. He realized that God saw him not as a sinner in need of punishment but as a luminous being worthy of infinite delight.

The journey into—and out of—the cave is one not only of self-discovery but of self-acceptance. We don't simply cut off that part of ourselves that might be tempted by the dark side; we accept it and love it and heal it. We don't suppress the shame or the doubt. We love our wounds into wholeness.

Saints and Jedi can surrender to shame and doubt, allowing them to forever control their destiny. Or they can muddle onward, mindful of their fears and temptations but determined to not allow those uncertainties to hold them back. So can we.

In the end, just as we needed to go *into* the cave, we also must *leave*. In this way, the shame that was holding us back can be exposed to the light. We cannot wallow in that shame.

Ignatius recognized that the enemy of our human nature likes to work in secret. Those evil spirits tend to flee when confronted by transparency and truth and openness. Our enemy "seeks to remain hidden and does not want to be discovered," Ignatius writes in his rules on discernment. The enemy "is greatly displeased if his evil suggestions . . . are revealed." Ignatius goes on to encourage us to find our own Yoda-figure to accompany us on our spiritual journey. He writes that if we share our struggles with another "spiritual person who understands [the evil spirit's] deceits and malicious designs," the evil one becomes "vexed." Evil prefers to operate under the cover of shadow.[35]

We leave the cave because there is more work to be done. Our lives continue. The meaning of our lives—and the mystery therein—goes on unfolding.

Fr. Burke reminded the pilgrims that the cave in Manresa was a place of *composition*. That's literally true; Ignatius *wrote* the *Spiritual Exercises* there. But it's also true in the sense that our stories continue to be written. The discoveries made in our personal caves are essential details in the stories we write from the lives that we live. We compose new chapters to propel our story.

Confident in this new knowledge, in this renewed sense of self and self-purpose, we set out from the darkness.

ONLY WHAT YOU TAKE WITH YOU

6. **Reach out.** Imagine a cave—or an equivalent space. Create it in your mind: rocky walls covered in ice; dirt; stones scattered across the ground; and cold darkness. Imagine yourself entering that space. What do you feel?

7. **Set your intention.** There is a need to confront darkness, to ferret it out and hold it to the light. We carry it within us—and that's okay. But we do so knowing we must push back against its hold on our very selves.

   Make your mantra by completing this sentence: *What I must rise above is . . .* what? Repeat that mantra several times. Be mindful of your breath.

8. **Review the past.** As you repeat your mantra, allow your mind to wander. Where does it go? Are you thinking of a moment from earlier today, earlier this year, or many years ago? Time in our proverbial cave can summon forth all sorts of uncomfortable memories, emotions, and feelings—and fears. Face them down; look at them directly. What moments bubble up that most clearly encapsulate how you feel?

   Settle on a single moment. What insight does this moment reveal to you?

9. **Always in motion.** The moment you've settled on from your past necessarily informs your present and might guide you into the future. Look at it— and smile. Because this, too, can be risen above. What do you need to practice in order to do so? Patience? Self-acceptance? Compassion? Perhaps you need a spiritual companion to accompany you.

10. **This is the way.** Darkness and evil flourish in shadow and secrecy. What has your time in the cave revealed? Who might you share these insights with so as to push back against this temptation to silence?

End your reflection by cultivating a disposition of gratitude to yourself, the universe, and the infinite Other.

CHAPTER 6

VISIONS

In the world of Jedi and Sith, visions are often dramatic. To us, they may seem like pure fantasy. Most likely, visions this extravagant are few and far between in our lives. But all the same, if we pay attention to the inner workings of our spiritual lives, we begin to detect gentle nudges, tugs, and invitations. We may not *literally* see things, but we do begin to get a sense of what might unfold if we choose one path over another. We can guess at the potential pitfalls and opportunities ahead, and we can make decisions on how to proceed with increasing confidence.

Does this sound like Jedi magic? It's not. In the Ignatian tradition, we talk about rules for discernment, which are spiritual practices and insights that allow us to better understand what's going on in our deepest selves. As we'll see in this chapter, there's much we can learn from "visions."

A VISION OF BELONGING

Ancient stone towers, nestled between the water and the forest on the picturesque world of Takodana, jut up from the shore of Nymeve Lake. Flags of all colors flying at the gate greet weary galactic travelers, and drink and companionship are a sure thing within.

Or at least that's how the old pirate Maz Kanata ran things before the arrival of the First Order. Before they bombed the place into a million little pieces of rock and dust.

But more than its appearance, the secrets hidden within the walls were the real draw of Maz's castle. That was why we moviegoers were brought to Takodana, right? Rey's visit was a pivotal moment in the plot of *The Force Awakens*.

She hears the screaming just after Finn leaves, when her only friend—and a brief friendship at that—was turning his back on the Resistance, on hope and justice in the galaxy, instead looking to protect only himself. Finn invited Rey to join him, to flee into the shadows of some distant planet and leave all this adventuring behind. But Rey had finally left Jakku. She had finally responded to that holy restlessness, to those swirling grains of sand, and now found herself swept up in something bigger, something important.

Sadly, she watched Finn pass through the doorway out of Maz's castle—and, seemingly, out of her life. Had she made the right decision? Her eyes betrayed uncertainty.

And then the screaming.

With the little round droid BB-8 in tow, Rey descends into the basement of the castle. Following the screams, she finds doors opening to her that should've been locked, and drops to her knees at the foot of a crate. She opens it. She peers inside.

She sees a lightsaber. She reaches out, slowly, hesitantly, and touches the hilt. She had no way of knowing that this was the lost lightsaber of Luke Skywalker and his father before him. That's when the powerful vision begins to unfold in a montage of terrifying images: glimpses of black-clad warriors wielding crimson lightsabers; an old man on his knees, reaching for his droid as flames burn all around him; voices whispering about Jedi and the Force and an energy field. Rey runs through hallways and darkened woods and finally comes face-to-face with a masked stranger who is bent on her destruction.

And then she stumbles back into the present moment. BB-8 rolls about worriedly, and Maz Kanata herself reaches out for Rey, offering the girl a hand of comfort.

Does Maz know what Rey has seen? Does she know what she's experienced? It's unclear. But what Maz *does* seem to know is that Rey must press on. Whatever she has seen is important.

"The belonging you seek is not behind you," Maz insists, seeing doubt in the girl's eyes. "It is ahead."

For a moment, it looks as though Rey will agree with the pirate. It appears that Maz's efforts at comfort and solace have succeeded. But then something in Rey's mind seems to change her resolve. She stumbles to her feet. She insists she wants nothing to do with any of this. And she flees the castle.

GOOD SPIRIT, BAD SPIRIT

Rey's Force vision is a great scene. I remember watching it for the first time in the theater. It had been ten years since new Star Wars stories were told on the big screen, not including the 2008 animated film. I heard Yoda's voice; I heard Obi-Wan. I recognized Luke and R2-D2. The sequence made me squirm with delight; *How cool!* But, of course, our hero Rey would react quite differently. For her, it wasn't a nostalgia-infused flashback. For her, it was terrifying.

For moviegoers in the theater that day, we knew that these scenes *should* have inspired Rey in her quest. *That's the voice of Alec Guinness and Ewan McGregor as Obi-Wan! Listen to them, Rey!* But what we moviegoers clearly saw as proof that Rey was on the right track was interpreted quite differently by the character herself.

That's par for the course in the spiritual life. Context matters. What one person perceives to be the work of a good spirit might rightly be viewed by another person as the mischief being made by a bad spirit. This is why it helps to have companions in the spiritual life, mentors to guide us in our decision-making and discernment. We all need a Maz.

Ignatius of Loyola spoke a lot about good spirits and bad spirits. He developed tools for discerning these spirits, for deciding which was acting on a person at any particular time. For Ignatius, the good spirit worked in a person's life in ways that would bring people closer to God's dream for them. The good spirit *desires* that we actively *engage* with the common good, that we *discover* peace and *work* for justice, that we *build* community and *forgo* temptations toward self-interest and self-promotion.

Bad spirits, on the other hand, want to see us isolated, cut off from our community, drowning in shame and self-rejection, and chasing after worthless idols and achievements that will not bring us true happiness or peace. Spelled out in this way, the discernment of spirits might sound easy. But, of course, we know from our own lives that sometimes what appears to be good actually delivers results that are bad for us, bad for our community, and bad for the world. So what to do? Again, context is key.

DISCERNING SPIRITS

Let me share an example from my own life.

As I was preparing to wrap up my undergraduate career at Fairfield University, I had two clear but divergent next steps. Somehow, I had been holding down a profitable internship in international tax at a big accounting firm. I was making more money than I had ever made. I was even offered a job to start at the firm in the fall—despite the fact that the only apparent qualification my Bachelor of Arts in creative writing and international studies seemed to grant me was that all-important word: international. Say it enough times and you can work in *international* tax, I told myself.

On the other hand, I had also been accepted into a postgraduate service program in Bolivia. I'd have a chance to put all those international studies courses to practical use, and I'd probably get a lot of great stories to write about. I'd make no money, of course, but this was the path I was always destined to walk, right? Wasn't that what I hoped would happen when I signed up to study international nonprofit work?

Neither of those options was inherently bad. But what would they mean for me in my particular context?

In college, I took nothing more than a personal finance course. Other than that one course, my entire transcript listed studies in writing and international studies. I wanted to learn Spanish, travel, and I'd been particularly excited at the prospect of living in Bolivia, a country that had always fascinated me. My then-girlfriend and (spoiler alert) now-wife had already opted to spend the following year in Ecuador, and the prospect of accompanying one another through similar experiences was an attractive one. And I did want to work for an international nonprofit one day. Wouldn't a year of service be the right next step?

It seemed as if all signs pointed toward Bolivia. But maybe that was just the easy answer. At times, we all get caught up in the flow of life, do what we think is expected of us, and drift with the current rather than actively swim. That's not always right or healthy. The antidote is discernment.

It became essential to interrogate *why* I was intrigued by these two options. Living and working in Bolivia would give me a chance to learn and grow. I hoped to add some value to the community that hosted me, and bring back their stories and insights as I pursued some career serving the common good. Words like *solidarity, justice, challenge,* and *authenticity* came to mind when I contemplated a year in Latin America. Thinking about this avenue left me feeling excited and hopeful, if a little uncertain and anxious.

Different words came to mind when I thought about that accounting job: *money, air conditioning, easy commute, easy transition.* This option left me feeling dry, hollow, and out of place.

I hadn't been preparing for a job in international tax; this wasn't my dream, what I had been working toward. For me, that was the wrong choice—though you can see how it could be the *right* choice for folks who *had* been studying tax law or dreaming up ways to apply business acumen to the common good. The words and feelings that washed over me when discerning between these two options were quite different than what I imagine such a person would experience.

And for good reason. Context matters. Good and bad spirits deal with us *as we are*, taking into account our past, our hopes, our fears, and our experiences.

THE DISCERNMENT SPONGE

St. Ignatius gives us clear and compelling imagery for differentiating between good and bad spirits at work in our lives:

> In souls that are progressing to greater perfection, the action of the good angel is delicate, gentle, delightful. It may be compared to a drop of water penetrating a sponge. The action of the evil spirit upon such souls is violent, noisy and disturbing. It may be compared to a drop of water falling upon a stone. In souls that are going from bad to worse, the action of the spirits mentioned above is just the reverse.[36]

What I always take from Ignatius's imagery is that the noisier spirit is trying to get our attention. But that's not always a good thing.

I realized quickly that what was most attractive about that job in international tax was the money, the comfort, and the prestige. These are all things that, in my context, pointed only to my own self-interest rather than to the common good I had spent my entire college career studying and preparing to contribute to. Once I realized this, I was able to see that a year of international service was the correct next step for me. This decision flowed naturally from the good patterns my life had already begun to reveal.

ARE WE AFRAID?

If we return to Rey's Force vision and her subsequent conversation with Maz, we can see more clearly that there were dueling spirits at work. Rey had left Jakku. She had finally embarked on this great adventure that was leading her toward something more. It had been hard for her, but things were falling into place: she had a mentor in Han Solo, a friend in Finn, a new purpose as a pilot, and a destination in the Resistance.

But then things became uncertain. That Force vision showed her a past she couldn't shake and a future that was terrifying. Loud and jarring and deeply unsettling, it shook her from the path that she had only recently committed to follow.

Maz's words of comfort almost put her back on track. But in the end, what she had seen and experienced—grounded in her own context, which is to say her own troubled past and mysterious future—sent her running for the woods.

The evil spirit—the dark side of the Force—won that round.

Fear, after all, is a tool of the dark side. Sudden bouts of fear that we aren't enough, will never be enough, are in fact imposters in our own lives, are the kinds of false visions that often are tools of the evil spirit.

It's hard—at times, even impossible—to shake such fears. But we don't need to be governed by them. We don't need to be distracted by them. Rather, we are challenged again to consider where we place our focus: Do we give our attention to that good spirit in our life, the one inviting us to become more fully our best selves, challenging though it may be? Or do we give our attention to the evil spirits stoking fear and shame and uncertainty? Do we allow ourselves to become paralyzed? Or do we push forward, even if but a single step?

VISIONS OF CLICKS, LIKES, AND COMMENTS

Few of us may have Force visions like Rey's, but there is no shortage of content with which to feed our senses. Consider, for example, something as simple and prevalent as social media. Is this the kind of *vision* you and I immerse ourselves in each day? And do we see things that frighten us? Things that call our sense of self into question? Things that distort truth and fact and plunge us into inner turmoil? Or do we seek out what nourishes us, builds us up, and clarifies our best selves?

Every day is a new day, and none of us get it right all the time. But the invitation of the good spirit is to continue on, to begin to grow comfortable with and accustomed to that gentle drop of water so as to infuse and expand our inner sponge.

And the work of the evil spirit? I'll bet each of us knows what it feels like to be spiritually dry. Bereft. Empty.

In such cases, pause, look around, turn back. Go slowly. This is no time to run reflexively and unthinkingly into the woods of Takodana. In such moments our vulnerable selves are not best able to deal with the Kylo Rens of our own lives.

DARKNESS AND LIGHT

Ignatius sees the spirits as always dueling, exactly as the dark and light sides of the Force are always tugging at our heroes. Tugging at us.

"Darkness rises and light to meet it," Snoke bellows in *The Last Jedi*. I love that line. It's so true. In the animated series *Star Wars: Visions Volume II*, in the short "Sith," we meet Lola, who gives us additional insight into that truth. She was once a Sith but now lives as a recluse and a painter. But she's troubled. "It's like darkness wants to be part of the painting," she says as droplets of paint stubbornly turn black.

When her former Sith master tracks her down, he insists that her fate *is* darkness. But Lola realizes something: "Light and darkness *are* part of the painting. Part of me." And those droplets of paint turn into all shades of color.

Light and dark are always present in our universe, in our lives, in our very selves. We don't defeat one in favor of the other. Both exist as constant forces in nature. We have to learn to live with that interplay.

What that means for our spiritual journeys is that when we fall to the dark side, when the evil spirit derails us, we always have the good spirit, the light side, to look to in order to regain balance and right ourselves. This was also true for Ignatius. The God he believed in was a God of perpetual compassion; no one is ever too far gone.

In the end, even if Rey made the wrong choice in that moment, she was given another opportunity to choose anew. And another after that. She overcame her fears, her sense of impostor syndrome, her own dark secrets. She defeated the Sith—at least, for a time. Her example shows us that we can too.

WAYFINDER EXERCISE

BELONGING AHEAD

1. **Reach out.** Clear your mind of all images, sounds, emotions. Try to hold on to a space of nothingness, emptiness. Is it possible? What presses in, attempting to distract your senses? What feelings well up in you as a result?

2. **Set your intention.** Consider the visions that appear in your own mind—throughout your waking hours, and even into sleep. Are they random, meaningless? Or is there something else at work here?

   Make your mantra by completing this sentence: *My senses show me* . . . what? Repeat that mantra several times. Be mindful of your breath.

3. **Review the past.** As you repeat your mantra, allow your mind to wander. Where does it go? Are you thinking of a moment from earlier today, earlier this year, or many years ago? Do any particular memories—let's call these our *visions*—come to the fore? What emotions accompany them? Do you feel that these moments led you deeper into your own sense of self or further away?

   Settle on a single moment. What insight does this moment reveal to you?

4. **Always in motion.** The moment you've settled on from your past necessarily informs your present and might guide you into the future. Is your sponge being filled or drying up?

5. **This is the way.** What do you need to do to ensure that you are spiritually nourished? Commit to a small but meaningful act.

End your reflection by cultivating a disposition of gratitude to yourself, the universe, and the infinite Other.

CHAPTER 7

EDITS

The 1997 special edition release of the original Star Wars trilogy caught a lot of flak. Something about messing around with a classic, tinkering about the edges with the accepted status quo, irked people, and ignited a global controversy over *who shot first* (more on that later). It was as if George Lucas had stuck his hand into our agreed-upon past—our childhoods, even—and rewrote history.

That's a pretty awesome power, if you can get it. And dangerous. How often do we look at our personal past, our collective past, and our national or international past and wish we could rewrite what happened? Delete the mistakes and retrace the missteps? Make ourselves out to be the heroes?

We see this temptation play out in the political arena, but it also plays out in our inner lives. We omit details of our past that are embarrassing, undermine our credibility, or make us feel uncomfortable. These defense mechanisms might be all right in certain situations. After all, there's no need to share with your barista a litany of past sins. But at our core, we need to engage with and embrace our *actual* past, shortcomings and all.

Sounds easy enough, right? It's not. The inclination to constantly edit our own stories and self-perception is always there. In this chapter, we'll reflect on why we need to confront this temptation head-on.

SPECIAL EDITION, OR UNENDING QUEST FOR PERFECTION?

I said it before and I'll say it again now: I liked the Star Wars special edition films. I grew up with them. My dad sat me down in our living room one night not long before their release, pulled out his VHS copies of the *original* saga, and away we went. I spent the next week immersed in a galaxy far, far away. This was just a year or so before Lucas's tinkered tales appeared on the big screen, so to me, "special edition" just meant *more* Star Wars. I was all in.

Of course, all this tinkering was Lucas's dry run for *The Phantom Menace*, an exploration of technology that was simply unavailable in the 1970s. He had one foot in the past and one in the future. But this idea of George Lucas as a tinkerer—someone constantly altering ever so slightly what has come before so as to perfect that which is and will yet be—has always appealed to me. The story stayed the same, mostly. He was just tinkering, poking at the edges of what was. He was still dreaming into completion what could be. He refused to be done, refused to settle. Refused to let reality fall short of the perfect story he dreamed of telling.

There's something spiritually compelling in Lucas's inability to let go. Familiar. A desire to keep returning, to keep improving in the hopes that this time, things will be different. This time, we'll get it right.

I brought this up on the weekly podcast I cohost, "AMDG: A Jesuit Podcast."[37] I thought I had just the right question. I knew where the deep end of the spiritual pool was to be found.

"What might we learn for the spiritual life from George Lucas's constant tinkering with his films?"

My guest's response was not what I expected. And as it turned out, I was at risk of drowning in that deep spiritual pool. "Well, Eric, I think we have differing takes on this," my guest said. "I hear what you're saying; I see what you're driving at. But I don't think it's a good thing. Lucas wasn't able to let go."

Ah—right. The anxious perfectionist in me *would* see an inability to let go of the past as a sign of virtue.

AN IGNATIAN CAUTION

Perfectionism *sounds* like a good thing.

There's a line in the Gospel of Matthew that goes like this: "So be perfect, just as your heavenly Father is perfect."[38] It haunts me. Perhaps it haunts you. This temptation to strive for perfection is, I think, a vice that masquerades as a virtue. It plagues the creative life, making the perfect an enemy of the good. But it's not just creatives who are impacted. This temptation eats away at our spiritual selves, too.

Still, it's not bad to want to improve, to learn from past mistakes, and fix those that can be mended. In fact, that's a really good thing! What we've learned in the present about the past can and should spur us to take steps toward reconciliation and justice. But this temptation to perfectionism is not always the same as a desire to work for justice and peace. Good and bad spirits are at work. How to tell the difference?

In his rules for discernment, and using imagery that was customary for his time and place, Ignatius of Loyola offers a helpful way to identify those dueling spirits. Ignatius talks of the "enemy of our human nature" as a military commander laying siege to our inner lives. The enemy studies our weak points so as to know when, where, and how to strike.

Where is there an open door in our spiritual selves that needs just a little push to let the darkness in? Is it that obsession over past mistakes? That desire to be perfect? Does this admirable-but-flawed desire leave us spiritually vulnerable? Speaking of the enemy, Ignatius writes, "Where he finds us weakest and most in need, there he attacks and tries to take us."[39] We know that we're under this proverbial siege when we find our otherwise good impulses resulting in bad outcomes: anger at our kids, snappiness toward our partners, self-loathing, shame, and paralysis. We get stuck in the past rather than learn from it so as to build a better future.

What's the answer?

Name it. Embrace your full self. If you know you have a temptation to perfectionism, it doesn't help to ignore or suppress it. The truth of the matter is, you'll never be able to edit out those parts of your story that make you cringe. There will be no special edition to your life.

HAN SHOT ~~FIRST SECOND~~ FIRST

The most notorious edit—and reedit and re-reedit—in *A New Hope* takes place in the Mos Eisley cantina. You know the place. It's the epitome of the scum and villainy that old Ben Kenobi disdains, a place of violence, greed, corruption, and gluttony.

At the center of it all is Han Solo. He owes Jabba the Hutt some money, and the gangster Hutt is ready to cash in. Enter Greedo, the green-skinned, big-eyed Rodian bounty hunter.

Greedo and Solo sit across the table from each other, deciding how best to navigate the situation. Is there more money to be made if Greedo hands Solo over to Jabba alive or dead? The bounty hunter makes no secret of the blaster he has pointed at Han.

Unfortunately for Greedo, Solo is a bit more subtle; Greedo never sees Solo remove his own blaster from his holster. And then he's dead. Solo rids himself of the troublesome bounty hunter with one quick shot, then pays the barkeep for the trouble on his way out.

But in subsequent releases of *A New Hope*, Greedo gets the first shot in. Rather than killing the bounty hunter in cold blood, Solo is made to appear as though he is simply responding in self-defense.

The fan base? Outraged. Thus, the global controversy: *Who shot first?*

The issue wasn't that Greedo got a shot off. Subsequent events in the movie weren't cast into chaos and confusion. The issue is that this small bit of tinkering changed the reputation of Han Solo.

There's a pivotal difference—legally, morally—between someone shooting someone else because the conversation has taken an unpleasant turn, and someone responding to an attack in self-defense. This feels less like an edit and more like an attempt at playing God, returning to an already-settled event in an effort to redeem a supposed character flaw.

This was probably meant to be a minor edit that just got out of hand. But it's illustrative of everything we're reflecting on in this chapter: We can't remake ourselves or others into past heroes. We can't tidy up events that have already unfolded, events that have already shaped us and the world. We can only learn from the past, deal with the present, and, in so doing, shape the future. Our wounds, both those we carry and those we've inflicted, cannot be undone. They can't be edited out. We must incorporate them, heal them, and move on.

THE PERFECTIONIST AT WORK

Obsessing over the past, and, in particular, over past *mistakes*, might seem like the right thing to do, especially within a religious context. How do we learn, if we don't recognize where we went wrong? Shouldn't we fix those past errors if we can?

Of course.

But instilling and encouraging shame, self-doubt, and constant reassessment leads not to growth but to spiritual paralysis. An earnest effort to *perfect* what has come before can easily lead us astray. Here's a simple example: When my wife and I moved into our new house, I wanted things to be perfect. I wanted the *house* to be perfect, and I wanted *to be* the perfect homeowner. There was work to be done, but I'm not a handy guy. So when I pulled out my drill and unfurled the instructions to hang up some hardware on the bathroom walls, it wasn't long before I had a hole in the wrong place and a stripped screw.

I nearly threw my drill through the bathroom mirror.

Now the *house* would be imperfect, and *I* was a failure. Every time I walked by that bathroom, I saw the crooked piece of hardware dangling from the wall. Even after the handyman fixed it, all I could think about for weeks was my insufficiency. I spent an inordinate amount of mental energy rehashing the mundane event: Had I drilled too aggressively? Should I have tried to jury-rig it myself? Would I have only made it worse, or proven myself as a homeowning wizard? What about the money spent on a handyman—had that been an unnecessary expense?

My wife told me to move on. I had other skills and, in fact, had managed to hang other things on the wall. It wasn't worth obsessing over; the end result was *good enough.*

Hanging a toilet paper holder on a piece of drywall is pretty low stakes. But zoom out. What mistakes have you made of real consequence, mistakes that have necessitated another person's involvement to correct? What proverbial hole have you left in the drywall of life? (How's that for prose?) How much mental energy have you spent rehashing those past events, and to what end? Mental, emotional, and spiritual energy devoted to the past is mental, emotional, and spiritual energy unavailable to you in the present.

I think of my two daughters, who are much better cared for when their dad isn't stressing over whether or not he hung the shelves right, or closed the basement window, or said just the right thing in that last email. When I'm a dad who's present to the moment, someone who is able to let go of past imperfections and instead love those little scoundrels who are right in front of me, everyone is much happier. And that sets them on a better path for their own futures.

SHOULD THE PAST DIE?

Although Kylo Ren insists we should let the past die, he is not able to follow his own advice. He's hell-bent on correcting his mistakes and suffers for it. He kills his father, an act that— rather than freeing him from the past—haunts him. He tries to kill his uncle, and, in that single-minded determination, fails, ultimately allowing the Resistance to be reborn, thwarting his own goals.

Ben Solo wanted to be the model Jedi. He wanted to impress his Master and uncle, Luke Skywalker. Luke tells a younger Ben in the novel *Shadow of the Sith*, years before the boy's transformation into Kylo Ren, "A Padawan offering to help his Master is an honorable gesture, but an unnecessary one."[40]

Ben retorts, "I might not be a Jedi Knight, but I'm stronger than you think." We see Ben's vulnerability, even if Luke does not. We see the dark side creeping in, pushing on that open door of insecurity. The Sith drew Ben toward the darkness and the supposed need to correct his past mistakes, his past shortcomings, to become what he wasn't able to be under Luke's tutelage.

Unfortunately, Ben didn't have Ignatius's rules for discernment. He didn't realize that those vulnerable places in his heart might be the very places that the dark side tries to break through.

The past doesn't need to die; it needs to be processed. It needs to be integrated. It needs to be accepted, made whole. And then the past needs to be left alone.

If we recognize our vulnerabilities, our perceived weaknesses, and love them anyway, bolstering them with some self-care rather than tearing them down with shame, the dark side will have that much harder a time breaking through.

WE CAN GET OUT

There's a powerful, poignant scene in the tenth episode of the first season of *Andor*. Cassian and his fellow inmates have finally mustered up the courage and designed a thorough enough plan to break free from the Imperial prison on Narkina 5. As they barrel down the hallways of the prison past Imperial officers cowering behind locked doors, they chant together, *One way out; one way out.*

The inmates were figurative cogs in a machine *building* literal cogs in a machine—the Death Star, to be specific. They were trapped in a sort of limbo, and we learned in the unfolding of the story that these unjustly imprisoned inmates were never going to be freed. The Empire was merely reassigning them to new cells. So they took matters into their hands; they seized an opportunity. They overpowered the guards. And they broke free.

But that scene—Cassian, Kino Loy, all the other inmates running, chanting, insisting on *one way out*—is illustrative. Quite simply, it's true. We can imprison ourselves in our own past, our own sins, our own missteps and regrets. We can idly spin mental cogs, never getting any closer to bettering ourselves or our world. Having never forgiven ourselves, never released ourselves from the need to be perfect, we waste away.

As we reflected on in the first part of this book, we may also find ourselves trapped in those larger structures of violence and injustice, our spiritual and emotional vulnerabilities taken advantage of by those systemic, unseen forces at work in society. Our mental prison is our literal and spiritual prison, and we toil away.

Or we can recognize that there's only one way out, only one way to go: Forward. Onward. In any case, allowing ourselves to waste away mentally, spiritually, or emotionally is no form of restoration or repentance. We may not be *perfect*, but we can continue to simply *be*—and therein lies our hope.

LET GO

I think back to the podcast interview and my guest, who said, "Perfectionism is part of what makes great art—and part of what ruins great art. The tendency to keep wanting to improve on something is a compulsion you'll never satisfy." He's right. Eventually, you have to let go.

The spiritual lesson to take from George Lucas's tinkering with Star Wars isn't that an obsession with perfecting what might have been is the best way forward. Rather, it's better to let go, accept what was, embrace the necessary limitations (for example, the technology of the 1970s), and recognize that what was in the past—good, bad, and ugly—is always with us. We are left to learn from our mistakes; suppressing or rewriting them leads nowhere productive and keeps us trapped in a past that is already beyond our grasp.

Instead, go deeper into the story. Draw new meaning from what came before so as to breathe new understanding into what exists now, right in front of you.

Keep telling the story. Add a new chapter. Give—*discover*—additional details, characters, insights. Isn't that what *Andor* and *Rogue One* did for *A New Hope*? Isn't that the whole point of the *From a Certain Point of View* short story anthologies? The original story is but a leaping-off point for bold, imaginative tales, an entryway through which we deepen our understanding of fascinating and classic characters. Imagine if we'd just kept tinkering with what was from 1977 rather than telling new tales that informed and deepened old stories. Imagine if those background characters just stayed there—in the background—rather than being given an opportunity to share their story. One path creates, ushering in new perspectives and insights and freedom; another path stymies, spinning old wheels in a well-worn patch of mud that only ensnares. The dark side would prefer we be stymied, that we fail to ever move forward.

We know, then, that the path of light is one in which we travel onward, not because we're fleeing from our mistakes but because, having lived through them, we can see who we are able to become.

ONE WAY OUT

1. **Reach out.** Settle into your space. Is there any tension or anxiety in your body? Reach for it; find it; name it.

2. **Set your intention.** This tension or anxiety might be the manifestation of some past frustration, worry, resentment, or regret. The tightness might be your body refusing to let go, a prison of sorts for some past mistake.

   Make your mantra by completing this sentence: *I will let the past . . .* what? Repeat that mantra several times. Be mindful of your breath.

3. **Review the past.** As you repeat your mantra, allow your mind to wander. Where does it go? Are you thinking of a moment from earlier today, earlier this year, or many years ago? Does this mental journey create or release tension in your body?

How might these many moments have gone unprocessed, unexamined? Do they continue to burden you? Do you spend mental energy trying to change what has already been done?

Settle on a single moment. What insight does this moment reveal to you?

4. **Always in motion.** The moment you've settled on from your past necessarily informs your present and might guide you into the future. Does your worry or obsession over this past mistake distract you from some good work that you are being invited to in this moment?

5. **This is the way.** Consider how the dark side (evil spirits) might be using your worries against you. Don't allow your focus to be stolen. Instead, choose something that fills you with joy, peace, and consolation.

End your reflection by cultivating a disposition of gratitude to yourself, the universe, and the infinite Other.

CHAPTER 8

TWO

The Dark Lords of the Sith have a rule: "Two there should be; no more, no less. One to embody power, the other to crave it."[41]

This instruction, articulated by Darth Bane in *Darth Bane: Path of Destruction*, a classic novel no longer *officially* considered canon, for those who worry about such things, is echoed in Master Yoda's own worried hand-wringing at the end of *The Phantom Menace*. He wrestles with the truth that Qui-Gon Jinn is dead at the hands of a Sith: "Always two there are," Yoda says. "A master and an apprentice."

The Jedi are rightly worried. Clouded, the future is, for the whole *purpose* of the ancient Sith philosophy is to mask the movement of these Dark Lords in secrecy until the time of their ultimate triumph. (Remember Ignatius's caution to be aware that evil desires shadow and secrecy, and hates being caught in the light?) And triumph the Sith do, as Maul's master, Darth Sidious (better known as Chancellor Palpatine), masterminds the downfall of the Republic and the Jedi Order, thereby enacting a reign of terror as the new Galactic Emperor.

There are times in our own spiritual lives when we feel as if our path is clouded. Powerful forces at play are mysterious and vague, and we struggle to discern what next steps we should take. That's the crossroads where Yoda and the entire Jedi Order stood in *The Phantom Menace*. Hindsight showed their choices to have been wrong.

But the Ignatian tradition gives us a tool to avoid the Jedi's unhappy fate. This tool is the pivotal meditation in the Second Week of the Spiritual Exercises. It's called the Two Standards, and it will guide us through this chapter.

MASTERS OF EVIL

Palpatine's master plan was a long time in the making; the Sith are patient and cunning. But the word in the Rule of Two that I find most illustrative is this: Crave. To crave something goes beyond simple wants or desires; it comes right up to the line of addiction. To crave is to *need* something—to need it for your very survival. And when the stakes become existential, when our very selves are at risk, we alter the course of our lives to make sure we get the thing that we think we need. Everything else fades from view and falls to the wayside.

What the Sith crave is *power.*

The Rule of Two is meant to end in the death of one: The *craving* for power is satisfied only once the apprentice has learned enough to overthrow the master. What kind of relationship is this? One in which the only person you can really trust is the person seemingly destined to destroy you. There's no real relationship there, only raw power and constant fear.

When, in *A New Hope*, Darth Vader faces off against Obi-Wan Kenobi on the Death Star, he's sure to tell his old friend that he is no longer a learner; Vader *is* the master now.

And then he strikes Kenobi down without a moment's hesitation, barely registering his counterpart's clear sacrifice. Old Ben's words ring true: Vader's blindness to the larger ideology that drives him—namely, the Rule of Two—has made him nothing more than a master of evil.

Vader thought he needed Kenobi dead to fully embody the power he sought. To fully claim his destiny. Old Ben thought the exact opposite. His was the path of self-sacrifice, of concern for others and the common good. After all, he wanted to see Luke escape and get on with his own destiny. Kenobi didn't need to demonstrate his power. He didn't need to cling to it. What old Ben did instead was give up his power freely—and with it, his life.

Power. The pursuit of personal glory. Fear and fearmongering. Suffering. Aren't these marks of the dark side?

Sacrifice. Relationship. Concern for others and the common good. That sounds like the light side to me.

Of course, these spiritual concepts are familiar to us; we choose between them each and every day, albeit in less dramatic fashion. But do we recognize when we act upon our cravings for power, glory, and riches? Do we know what drives us? And how might we instead strive for the light? These questions are important as they affect not only individual decisions but also, over time, the very trajectory of our lives.

CHOOSING BETWEEN STANDARDS

The meditation on the Two Standards feels as if it belongs in a space fantasy. Ignatius invites us to imagine two warring parties, clashing on the field of battle. The huge armies are arrayed as far as the eye can see. Past battles have been fierce; future skirmishes promise nothing less. Each side holds a standard—imagine a banner or flag that represents each gathered force.

And there you are in the middle. You must choose.

On the one side, you see a powerful force that manifests itself in its thirst for riches, honors, and power. The soldiers in this army are after those things; it's what their leader has promised them. (Think: the Nihil from the High Republic era of Star Wars.) But as a result, they're always looking over their shoulder, worried that someone *else* has more riches, someone *else* is more respected. Despite being part of a group, each member of this force is out for themselves. How can they not be, when there are always more riches and honors to claim? There can only be one who is truly the most powerful, the richest, the most revered.

On the other side, you see a force that manifests itself by the search for poverty, humility, and rejection. These things sound unappealing, but those who gather around this standard appear to be more of a community, more of a team. Even though they claim to be seeking the specific virtues of poverty, humility, and rejection, these folks are really all about self-sacrifice, emptying themselves of ego and pride, and making themselves more available to the needs of others. As a result, companionship forms. Love blossoms. There is a recognition that they need one another. They cannot go it alone. The bonds between individuals and the foundation of the community are far stronger.

Peculiar armies? Perhaps. What if you imagined the former clad in dark, hooded cloaks wielding bloodred laser swords, lurking in the shadows of society, waiting to pounce and prosper? What if you imagined the latter clad in brown robes, an order of space monks endeavoring to discover and commune with the mystical energy force that connects all things?

Ignatius calls the path of riches, honors, and pride the Standard of the Enemy. He calls the path of poverty, humility, and rejection the Standard of Christ. We might as easily call them the dark side and the light.

I once attended a creative writing workshop facilitated by a professor who did not like Star Wars.

"It's too black and white," he grumbled. "Literally. Darth Vader emerges, and you *know* he's the villain. He's completely evil. And then Luke Skywalker—he's the hero, all good. There's no gradation. It's not true to life."

It won't surprise you to know I found this professor's take to be ridiculous. The Star Wars universe, just like our own, is full of gray. And characters are constantly moving along a continuum between the dark and the light. As are we.

The Two Standards, though they sound static and obvious, are anything but. Rather than imagine yourself joining one side and staying there forever, thus perfectly embodying good or evil for all time, think of the Standards as guideposts on the spiritual journey. The Standards *point the way* to a cause that is bigger than you or me. We can't possibly hope to embody that cause all the time. Think of the pressure! We can only hope to serve the good, the light—and recognize that which is evil and dark for what it is.

There would be hardly any conflict in Star Wars if every Jedi constantly, faithfully, and without question lived up to the Jedi Code. Simply *becoming* a Jedi doesn't mean you're in the clear. The life and legacy of a Jedi is built or broken by daily decisions.

Each decision we make becomes an opportunity to ask ourselves whether it will further the cause of good or the cause of evil. While that may sound obvious, we know from the muddied day-to-day of real life that easy, ordinary decisions often have unforeseen consequences. The Clone Wars, after all, first appear to the Jedi as the only path to uphold justice and peace in the galaxy. But in the end, the effort undermines and unravels their very Order—an Order hailed as one of peace. The Two Standards might have given the Jedi insight. It's helpful to layer in the riches/honors/pride framework versus the poverty/humility/rejection framework.

"There will be three steps," Ignatius writes. "The first, poverty as opposed to riches; the second, insults or contempt as opposed to the honor of this world; the third, humility as opposed to pride. . . . These three steps [lead] to all other virtues."[42]

Clearly, when we step *toward* poverty, the majority of us don't *actually* embody that poverty (though some might be called to do so). Rather, we take these steps thinking about what's driving us: Are we too attached to riches? Are we in it only for the money? Are we terrified of going without? We ask questions like these, and then we act.

We don't always get it right. But the thing about the Two Standards is that we continually have the opportunity to make new decisions that draw us either closer to or further from our intended destination.

STANDARDS FOR WRITING

This all might sound a bit vague. Let me give a specific example.

I love to write.

I've loved writing for a long time. As a teenager, I used to write fantasy stories—elves and dragons and quests, that sort of thing—and share them with my grandmother, herself an established travel writer. Throughout high school I read and I wrote, and I wrote what I wanted to read. I wound up studying creative writing in college, and writing has played an increasingly important role in my career ever since.

As I've aged, I've found the process of writing to be a way to pray. It's a way to discover things about myself and the world. It's a form of self-reflection. I write about things that are important to me, the fruit of my own prayer and experience: stories of my family, my struggles, my encounters with sorrow, suffering, and hope. As is the case for any creative endeavor, the personal and the professional bleed together.

As my writing gets read by more and more people, further self-reflection is demanded: Am I writing what people need to hear or solely what is easy to say? Are my words serving a purpose or simply myself? Does my craft contribute to the common good or does it become an exercise in mere self-promotion? In the spiritual writing I often do, it's easy to get caught up in personal storytelling for the sake of personal storytelling, or, even worse, mere pontificating. It's incumbent upon me, the writer, to strike the right balance, to share enough of myself so as to help the reader relate while still elevating the piece *beyond* my specific experience to be relevant and meaningful.

My readers let me know when I've missed the mark.

For many years, I've written a weekly column on applying Ignatian spirituality to everyday life. It's called *Now Discern This*. I share a story—like how I didn't pack enough food for a camping trip, or how my eldest daughter is always ready to host a princess party, or how we once saw the remains of an entire whale's spine in Iceland—and then I try to draw some spiritual meaning from it. The column goes out in email form, and I wait.

Every week, readers write back with their own reflections. Sometimes they share their own stories; sometimes they affirm mine. Sometimes they tell me how what I said was *just* what they needed to hear at that moment. At other times, they tell me that I share too many stories about my kids.

Regardless, I hear *something* each week. It helps me ensure that my writing is on track and meeting real needs of real people. If it's not, I can course correct.

But something more insidious happens, too. I wait for—or I might as well admit, I *crave*—praise. I want that self-affirmation. I know that at least once a week I'll be showered with kind words, notes from people saluting my writing and my insight and expressing gratitude for my work, my unique contribution. And while these things aren't bad in and of themselves—and in fact are useful when they help me improve my writing and storytelling—you can see where my gratitude for the kind words of others can slowly morph into an unhealthy addiction to affirmation, affection, and praise.

It becomes even more toxic when my writing is shared on social media. How often do I check to see how many likes or comments I've received, or if my writing has been shared? It's easy to become absorbed, refreshing social media sites and email inboxes in search of an ego boost. Often, this happens at the expense of projects and people—my children, my wife, my friends.

Does this dynamic sound familiar? Perhaps you're a creative of some kind; perhaps you simply post photos of your daily life on social media. Regardless, do you sense that *craving* that sinks into your relationship with work? With others?

Think of Ignatius's Standard of the Enemy—the dark side, if you will. Likes on social media, the sharing of your creative content, even the simple circulation of a good idea you had around the office—these aren't bad things in and of themselves. But you can see how quickly your attitude toward these things can change: Are you sharing this content, these ideas, for the greater good of society, or for your own aggrandizement?

It is easy to find yourself less concerned with the idea and more concerned with the credit. There is money to be gained, after all, from a good idea, a good piece of writing. And people rightly praise such work. Which leads to more work, more prestige, and the ability to produce more and earn more.

The more you have, the more you crave. Because, after all, you can never have enough, right? There is always someone richer, cooler, more powerful than you. There is always someone to beat—if your approach is a zero-sum battle in which you continually seek to store up riches, honors, and power to benefit your own pride.

From his book *The Extraordinary Gift of Being Ordinary*, psychologist Dr. Ronald D. Siegel writes, "Self-esteem boosts fit the addictive pattern perfectly. Whether it's getting likes on social media, buying that new car, having our team win, falling in love, or thinking we're a saint, we feel great—briefly. But soon we either habituate to our new status, slip down a rung, or become exhausted trying to keep from slipping. What's the solution? It's finding another boost, of course! Ad infinitum."[43]

That's the dark side. The Enemy's Standard. Yoda says it clearly: "Fear leads to anger. Anger leads to hate. Hate leads to suffering." We fear to come in second or third or last. We fear to fall from grace or to be found wanting. Our own lacking makes us angry—at ourselves, others, and the world. And when we are stuck in a fog of rage, we make everyone miserable. That's the trap.

In *Revenge of the Sith*, Yoda counsels Anakin Skywalker to train himself to let go of all the things he fears to lose. That is good advice for us, too, and it mirrors the path of Ignatius's Standard of Christ. In this way, we step out of the cycle of suffering. If we hold all things lightly, we cling to nothing. We have nothing to lose and thus nothing to fear.

We empty ourselves so as to be available to the needs of others and our world. "People who seek external rewards such as fame, power, wealth, and beauty in pursuit of popularity have more anxiety, depression, and discontent—long-term pain," Siegel writes. "Those who seek close, caring relationships, pursue personal growth, and enjoy helping others—intrinsic rewards and qualities associated with likability—tend to be happier and physically healthier."[44]

That's as relevant to me as a writer as it is to you in your own vocation as it is to a Jedi Master.

THE FORCE IS WITH ME

We know the Jedi grow complacent, locked away in their temples. They're easily manipulated into committing violence against others during the Clone Wars, all under the guise of maintaining a broken status quo. Even though their goals were peace and justice, they became too focused on maintaining power. They failed to see the stakes—the consequences of their ongoing actions—clearly. In the end, the Sith, manipulating the power of the Jedi for their own sinister ends, overthrew them.

Star Wars, though, isn't the story of those who have power; it's the story of those who have none. Rebellion, resistance, struggle. Our heroes succeed when they work together, when they oppose the Rule of Two through their actions and sacrifices.

As we end this chapter, let's reflect on the character of Chirrut Îmwe, first seen in *Rogue One: A Star Wars Story*. Chirrut has no power, no innate ability to call upon or wield the Force. He is but a humble Guardian of the Whills. He is poor, blind, spat upon by the Empire, and reliant on his one friend, Baze Malbus, for protection and guidance.

Despite all this, the following mantra is constantly on Chirrut's lips: "I am one with the Force; and the Force is with me." His faith in the Force is more impressive than that of the Jedi who have the raw power of the Force to wield. Chirrut has only his trust in that mystical energy field, his friends, and his skill with a lightbow to rely upon.

And yet, Chirrut never falters. He encourages his fellow rebels, inspires new faith in his old friend Baze, and ultimately plays a pivotal role in securing the Death Star plans during the Battle of Scarif—an act of self-sacrifice for the good of the many.

And all that without craving any real power at all.

Always Two There Are

1. **Reach out.** Imagine those two warring parties, one bearing the standard of light, the other bearing the standard of darkness. You gaze upon the battle, and your place therein appears obvious.

2. **Set your intention.** But as you study the opposing forces, you realize something: All is not as it appears. You sense deception in the air.

   Make your mantra by completing this sentence: *The path I walk is marked by . . .* what? Repeat that mantra several times. Be mindful of your breath.

3. **Review the past.** As you repeat your mantra, allow your mind to wander. Where does it go? Are you thinking of a moment from earlier today, earlier this year, or many years ago? How does the marking that clearly demarcates your life's path compare to the markings you see on the two warring standards? How do the moments that bubble up in your mind fit in with your understanding of the standards of light and dark?

   Settle on a single moment. What insight does this moment reveal to you?

4. **Always in motion.** The moment you've settled on from your past necessarily informs your present and might guide you into the future. You realize

that continuing along this path will bring difficulty. How tempting is it to turn aside and walk the other road? What would convince you to do so?

5. **This is the way.** Remember this: you do not walk alone. Who are the people in your life to best accompany you on this journey? Who are you invited to accompany? How does this community help you maintain the light and resist the temptation of the dark?

End your reflection by cultivating a disposition of gratitude to yourself, the universe, and the infinite Other.

PART 2 REPRISE

DARKNESS RISES; LIGHT MEETS IT

The *Empire Strikes Back* ends on a markedly different beat than *A New Hope*.

Gone is the celebratory pomp and circumstance that followed the destruction of the Death Star. There are no medals to be awarded, no smiles between heroes. There is no great triumph of the forces of good over evil. Rather than spin off into space in his TIE Advanced starfighter, this time around, Darth Vader has the last word, and Luke is left short one hand and wondering at the truth of his own family lineage. Han Solo is trapped in carbonite and in the company of bounty hunter Boba Fett and, as a result, our heroes scatter to lick their wounds. If ever there was a new hope, it seems to have all but dried up. Where's Dash Rendar when you need him?

"I analyzed *Empire* before production and came to the obvious conclusion that it was not just a sequel, but the second act of a three-act space opera," said Irvin Kershner, *Empire*'s director. "Now, the second act does not have the same climax as the third act or even the first act. The second act is usually more ambiguous. It is quieter, but the problems are accentuated; you get into depth. . . . It is about revealing character."[45]

In this way, *The Last Jedi* followed the example of *The Empire Strikes Back*. The Resistance is routed at Crait; Jedi Master Luke Skywalker sacrifices himself; and no one comes to Leia's aid. Hope, again, seems all but lost. The problems are certainly accentuated amid the deafening quiet of the galaxy's response.

As we come to the end of the second portion of this book, you might be having similar feelings. This part of our spiritual journey is necessarily different from the first. How exciting it was to identify the spiritual awakening within ourselves over the course of the initial chapters! To sink into our own desires, to identify opportunities to overcome injustices, to recognize that a simple change in focus can reveal wondrous new possibilities.

But now, we've been left grappling with the dueling forces of light and darkness within ourselves. We still may be trapped within our own caves, or struggling to discern which spirits are at work in our lives. We see the warring spirits all around us, and it can feel overwhelming. It's easier, certainly, to ignore this invitation to brave new spiritual depths.

Kershner's words are spiritually prophetic. This part of the spiritual journey—and we circle back to it again and again throughout our lives—is about character. It's about figuring out who we really are and who we are in community. Do we respond to the challenge of evil and darkness in our personal lives, thus preparing ourselves to address such evil in the wider world? Do we allow ourselves to live in the ambiguity, recognizing that it can be anything but simple to discern good from bad once we start muddling through the gray nature of our daily existence?

What's perhaps most important about Kershner's reflection on a three-part space opera is the basic fact that the second part is not the third. We aren't done yet.

Snoke's remark in *The Last Jedi* that if and when darkness rises, light does not hesitate to meet it, proves prophetic, too—but we have to believe it. We have to have the audacity to hope that it's true. That even in the darkest of moments—when the Rebel Fleet is scattered, when the Resistance is broken, when the entire galaxy is on the verge of being engulfed in the Clone Wars, when our heroes are bruised and battered and ready to give up—light remains.

Light remains *within us*. And we are enough to meet this darkness, to engage it head-on and call it what it is. In so doing, we prepare ourselves to begin the final portion of this spiritual journey.

PART 3

DISCERNING
A NEW HOPE

One chilly evening in late October, my friends and I sat down to watch a couple of movies about Ewoks— *Ewoks: Caravan of Courage* and *Ewoks: Battle for Endor*. It was my birthday party—a sleepover, no less—and I had just discovered these hidden gems at the local Blockbuster.

Man, was I going to be a hero.

Not *only* had I summoned from the void *new* Star Wars content for my gaggle of lightsaber-wielding buddies, but I had done so in a context in which there was also cake. The night was only going to get awesome.

Suffice it to say, a hero I was not.

Our return to the forest moon was one of raised eyebrows and general confusion. The Ewok movies are a bit of a mess. Fun? Sure. But I don't think they won a lot of awards.

All the same, I still bought copies on DVD as a testament to my love of Star Wars and as a tangible reminder of a genuinely fun birthday party. I proudly display the DVD cases alongside my other copies of Star Wars films and have done so for years.

Which is how, more than two decades later, my four-year-old daughter wound up with a DVD in her hand and a quizzical look on her face. This was during those long days of the stay-at-home pandemic.

"Is this me?" she asked, holding up the DVD case and pointing to the curly-haired five-year-old on the cover. The young protagonist of that strange duology, Cindel Towani, played by Aubree Miller, *did* look a whole lot like my daughter. Round face. Blonde curls. Big eyes.

"Uh . . ." I stammered.

My wife laughed. "You do look alike . . . but no."

My daughter didn't laugh. She just stared at the cover, seemingly trying to remember when she'd been cast in a film and forced to fight alongside spear-wielding teddy bears. (She wasn't that far off. She might have been having foggy memories of her first in-theater movie experience—*The Last Jedi*—when she was barely a month old.)

Honestly, that sort of immersive plunge into a world of fantasy—the belief that she really *was* that character—is what I wish for my daughters. It expands the imagination and allows us to push the boundaries of what we deem possible. If we can conjure up a moon covered in dense vegetation and inhabited by not only Ewoks but also a whole mess of other mysterious creatures, then who knows what else we can imagine? As a result, do we approach our day-to-day with greater creativity, greater humility, greater possibility?

Sure, we don't expect to bump into Ewoks. But maybe we expand our expectations—or drop them altogether.

Maybe we allow ourselves to be surprised and delighted by the proverbial spear-wielding teddy bears in our own lives.

That's the mentality I brought to parenting during those pandemic months. I was determined to immerse my young daughters in my love of Star Wars. One way I did that was by inviting my eldest to join me in building all sorts of Star Wars LEGO sets.

This wasn't just an exercise in imagining the fantastical. This was an exercise in actually creating it. Bringing it to fruition, one piece at a time. Which, of course, is what we're all called to do each and every day: usher into existence a better, more colorful, more magical world.

Spirituality made manifest.

We find ourselves in a similar place at this point in our journey. We have awakened to the spiritual realities around us. We have engaged the dueling spirits at work in our lives. We know the stakes. To paraphrase Ben Kenobi, we've either taken our first steps into a larger world or, more likely, we've taken *more* steps. New steps. Intentional steps. We want to figure out what to do next, how to engage the spiritual life in a way that is meaningful to the nitty-gritty reality of our everyday experiences—and the communities in which those experiences take place. We want to rediscover and make real the hope that seems to fade in the shadows of sorrow and suffering.

That's what the next and final part of this book is all about: How do we manifest this disposition of hope to the world? Because it *is* hope we're talking about. It isn't a *hopeless* person who decides to get up in the morning and keep going, keep working, keep striving for even tiny, seemingly insignificant improvements to life and the common good.

Hope sustains us, pushes us forward, inspires us to keep putting one foot in front of the other, even when we think it's all but abandoned us, all but run out.

Hope is what we bring with us when we return to a well-worn story: the hope to discover something new, to find solace in something old. Hope is what a gaggle of preteen boys brought to a sleepover-bound-movie about Ewoks: *What's this new chapter in an old story have to say?* And it's what a little girl and her father bring to a pile of plastic bricks: *What experience might we create and imagine together?*

Hope demands action. Hope is built upon practice, and it breeds a disposition. Hope in a future that has yet to be imagined, that's worth working for, that's worth upsetting the status quo over, is what separates rebels from stormtroopers.

Hope is what we bring to the questions of greatest importance. What might we find here, now, in this place, that we might make use of tomorrow?

And so, as we near the end of this journey, we reflect on what it means to practice and sustain hope. We explore spiritual concepts like indifference and redemption, and we discern the potential for spiritual institutions and pilgrimages. How do these things help us manifest hope for others and for ourselves? In the end, we ask how we can put what we've learned from our own spiritual quests at the disposal of the greater good.

May the Force be with us.

CHAPTER 9

INDIFFERENCE

There's an argument to be made that it's actually R2-D2 who is the Rebellion's only hope.

Think back to the original Star Wars film: we're barely ten minutes into *A New Hope*, and things are looking pretty dire for C-3PO and R2-D2, our battered droid heroes.

Their ship, the *Tantive IV*, has been attacked, boarded, and overrun by the Empire. The crew is lost; their master, the princess of Alderaan, captured. This follows immediately on the heels of the Battle of Scarif, where rebel soldiers were cut down left and right. And now, in the wake of battles and escape pods, our droid duo is muddling about the dunes of Tatooine.

It's no wonder C-3PO thinks he and his counterpart are made to suffer. Who in 3PO's metallic shoes *wouldn't* gripe and complain and search for the easiest route back to safety and sanity?!

But R2-D2, much to his golden counterpart's chagrin, thinks differently. He heads straight into the desolate depths of the Tatooine desert, leaving 3PO to throw up his hands in weary frustration and abandon R2 to his delusions of grandeur.

We know that R2-D2 carries within him the plans to the Death Star as well as its hidden weakness. This is the knowledge for which countless rebels—from Jyn Erso to Cassian Andor to Raymus Antilles—gave their lives. In the face of a planet killer, an evil that could alter the course of galactic history, what this little droid carries within him is no less than hope itself.

C-3PO may not have been privy to R2-D2's hidden agenda, and it's no surprise as to why. The golden protocol droid gets flustered easily, and his default mode is an assumption of impending doom. Though he rises to meet the moment on many an occasion, C-3PO does not possess the flexible determination of R2-D2, who just keeps rolling with the punches. Changing context rarely seems to phase R2-D2.

In *The Phantom Menace*, R2 single-handedly repairs the damaged Naboo Royal Starship, undaunted by both the dogfight going on all around him and the destruction of his fellow astromech droids. He knows his purpose, his skill set, and what is expected of him. He meets the moment as best he can.

From space to sand, R2 *does* what he *is*. There is seemingly no gap between his identity and his purpose. He carries on, undeterred, ever focused on the mission of the moment. He, in fact, does *not* have delusions of grandeur; he is focused instead on what is expected of him and on what he can *actually* accomplish.

He both carries and manifests hope. And he resists the temptation to dwell in suffering, doom, and regret. Learning from R2's example, we'll spend this chapter reflecting on how we, too, can *do* what we *are*, using tools from Ignatian spirituality, as well as parallel practices I've found helpful in Daoism and Buddhism.

PRACTICE INDIFFERENCE

The Ignatian tradition elevates a peculiar virtue: Indifference. This is no glorification of apathy or nihilism but rather a spiritual path to channeling passion, energy, and purpose. Indifference means detachment from our own preferences, comforts, and expectations so as to achieve the freedom to act for the good. Here, picture little R2 rolling along in that Tatooine sand, unconcerned with the heat of the sun or the glory of success, refusing to give in to the seeming hopelessness of the situation, but focused solely on the good to be accomplished in the present moment.

The prolific Ignatian writer Jim Manney in his book *What Do You Really Want?: St. Ignatius Loyola and the Art of Discernment,* explains that indifference "means impartiality and objectivity, not a cold lack of concern. It means we hold all of God's gifts reverently but also lightly, embracing them or letting them go depending on how they help us fulfill our vocation to love in the concrete circumstances of our lives. . . . [It] means that we are free from personal preferences, societal expectations, fears of poverty and loneliness, desires for fame and honor, and anything else that has a hold on us."[46]

As we've already seen, Ignatius of Loyola was keen on helping people identify and act upon God's will in and for their lives. For Ignatius, this is key to the Spiritual Exercises in particular and the spiritual life in general. It's how the Exercises begin—in the First Principle and Foundation introduced at the outset, we pray "to make ourselves indifferent to all created things"[47]—and it's expressed in the *Suscipe* Prayer at the conclusion of the Exercises. This disposition of indifference for freedom is "a stance of openness to what God wants, which is what we most deeply want as well," Manney says.[48]

This language might make us feel uncomfortable. I confess that I raised more than an eyebrow when I first encountered this bit of Ignatian spirituality. "Conform myself to the will of God?" I thought. "That sounds limiting at best and infantilizing at worst. I think for myself!" I hope by now in this book, you think of the *will of God* differently. In the Venn diagram of the spiritual life, the will of God and our deepest desires are two perfectly overlapping circles.

In any case, we need to abandon any view of God as an old dude in the clouds directing affairs of the universe like a theater stage manager. Instead, we need to see the will of God as the very fabric and force of the universe, a constant flow of that which is holy ushering us onward, further and further into our deepest selves. As my spiritual director Fr. James Bowler, SJ, whom I met during my undergraduate studies at Fairfield University, has reminded me, the will of God is experienced in the very process of evolution, a constant drawing forth from all of creation that which is expressive of creation's own full flourishing. The will of God in our lives is the discovery and actualization of our own greatest purpose within a particular context, interconnected with all things.

Still. This idea of God's will and our participation in it. . . . Believe it or not, I came to understand it best by approaching it through the language of a completely different religious tradition.

THROUGH A DIFFERENT DOOR

When I was an undergraduate student, I took a course titled "Philosophical Daoism and Zen Buddhism." I know what you're thinking: *Look at this guy! He took one course when he was nineteen years old, and now he thinks he knows everything about Zen Buddhism and Daoism.*

To that I say, *Don't get sassy.*

But it was a significant moment. It came when I was a second-year student. I was in a living and learning community that sought to form us in Ignatian spirituality. The prevailing philosophy was that Ignatian spirituality—really, any spiritual path—benefits from and is informed by other spiritual traditions. Fr. Bowler told me that I would do well as a Catholic to immerse myself in and learn from a spiritual and religious tradition that was different from my own. I listened to his advice, and I took that class seriously. To this day, the tenets I was able to take away from that course continue to inform how I approach the world and how I approach spirituality.

Now, it must be clarified: I am not saying all religions or spiritualities are the same. They're not. Religious traditions emerge from and continue to grow within specific contexts. They propose distinct ways for people to become fully flourishing beings. They grapple with the world in very different ways, and diagnose human suffering in divergent manners. But I do believe that, regardless of whether you have a spiritual practice or religious tradition, there is more you can learn about your *own* beliefs by reflecting on those of another. Enter through a different door and discover a marvelous truth: each of our traditions has something unique yet analogous to say about our shared human experience. We all stare into the same mirror, though in this life that mirror is clouded (1 Cor 13:12).

So let's see what Zen Buddhism, Daoism, and Ignatian indifference can teach us about our own spiritual paths.

R2-D2, ZEN MASTER

In his delightful book *The Zen of R2-D2*, Matthew Bortolin takes us to Cloud City. Remember that chaotic escape scene in *The Empire Strikes Back*? Following his defeat by Darth Vader, Luke has just been saved and Lando, Chewbacca, and Leia are eager to get the *Millennium Falcon* well away from the approaching Star Destroyer. Unfortunately, when the moment to accelerate to light speed comes, we hear nothing but the whine of failing systems.

Things look bad. Everyone races to figure out a solution.

But R2-D2 knows the problem: the hyperdrive has been deactivated. He learned as much from Cloud City's central computer while he was plugged into it. So he knows how to fix the problem, and fix it he does—quickly, efficiently, with little fuss.

People who embody Zen, Bortolin writes, "see clearly and then they act appropriately . . . because they live lives of direct experience."[49] R2, simply by being what he is, by doing what he does, is able to perceive what is needed of him in that moment. He isn't looking for possible problems with the *Falcon*; he is simply always aware. His past choices flow perfectly into his present situation, allowing the future to unfold for others. "When your head isn't filled with the usual noise, you've got plenty of space for the unexpected to come your way—and you can recognize its value when it does."[50] Remember how important it is to practice mindfulness? Of being deeply aware of what's going on all around you?

This sense of *flow* is key to what we're talking about. If you imagine yourself in a river, do you allow the current to guide your body, even though you're bumping over rocks and getting bruised by debris, rushing onward toward the great lake beyond? Or do you waste time and energy grasping at things—that dangling vine, that protruding root, that enormous boulder—in an effort to resist the inevitable flow of the water?

Is the universe flowing in a similar way? Once we've found our path, would we do better to ride that flow, to allow it to wash over us and bring us to our necessary destination? Or should we stand against it? Do we hold things tightly or loosely? How much faster might we reach our destination if we could tap into that flow of the universe!

THE PRACTICE OF NONACTION

In Daoism, the closest reflection of both Ignatian indifference and this concept of flowing Zen is wu wei, often translated as "nonaction." Wu wei is a teaching of Lao Tzu, whom many believe is the founder of Philosophical Daoism as well as the author of the essential Daoist text, *Tao Te Ching.* The Eastern Orthodox monk Hieromonk Damascene offers an important disclaimer on wu wei in *Christ the Eternal Tao,* his Christian take on the *Tao Te Ching.* "Some have wrongly interpreted Lao Tzu's wu wei to mean 'doing nothing at all,' but this is far from its intended meaning."[51]

Thomas Merton was a Catholic and Trappist monk who devoted much time, study, and reflection to spiritual traditions quite different from his own. Merton writes eloquently on this topic in his book *The Way of Chuang Tzu*:

> The true character of wu wei is not mere inactivity but *perfect action*—because it is act without activity. In other words, it is action not carried out independently of Heaven and earth and in conflict with the dynamism of the whole, but in perfect harmony with the whole. It is not mere passivity, but it is

action that seems both effortless and spontaneous because performed "rightly," in perfect accordance with our nature and with our place in the scheme of things. It is completely free because there is in it no force and no violence. It is not "conditioned" or "limited" by our own individual needs and desires, or even by our own theories and ideas.[52]

There is both the abandonment of self and, paradoxically, an embracing of my uniqueness. We choose to empty ourselves of the stuff that is *me* in favor of allowing ourselves to be filled with the stuff of the universe. Of God. Of that which is holy and sacred.

Each of us are part of this universe. We contribute something unique and vital *if* we are able to get out of our own way and allow that contribution to take place. Can we tap into that flow, that nonaction, and *be* who and what we are? Can we allow our unique selves to go beyond our own limitations and connect with the wider universe?

"When we raise our awareness to the level of our spirit, and there seek the Divine Spirit, we begin to find the still Source of the non-action of which Lao Tzu speaks," writes Damascene. "We abandon our erroneous trust in our thoughts and feelings and instead trust the Divine Source of truth. When this awareness informs our actions, we will be practicing . . . nonaction."[53] In Damascene's words, we glimpse again the idea of the *will of God* and the importance of discerning spirits.

We already know that our feelings and desires and passions can be either manifestations of that Divine Source or a trick of the enemy of our human nature. One leads us astray.

The other conforms us to wu wei and allows us to sink more deeply into the larger project of humanity. We contribute our part while doing nothing other than simply being who we are made to be.

A less lofty example: Imagine you're playing an instrument. You lose yourself in the music. The music *flows* out of you, and you barely register the act of playing. This is being in a state of wu wei. It also, as Bortolin writes, is Zen. You experience life free from self-concept "when the distinction between your 'self' and the activity you are engaged in disappears." Your mind "is alert and active but it has stopped rehashing the past and labeling the present and planning the future. It is just aware. . . . There is no 'you' in that moment. And yet there you are."[54]

INDIFFERENT, NOT DEFEATIST

It's tempting to look at these concepts of indifference, nonaction, and Zen and assume that the answer to the spiritual life is to throw up our hands and let things run their course. Suffering is not just inevitable but perhaps even part of the plan. That's not it at all. Rather, I hope you read these words as an invitation to go deeper, to discover the hidden river pulsing just beneath the surface of your spiritual life. Ignatian spirituality challenges us to discern the will of God not so that we can look at the suffering and hardship in the world and assume that God wills it, but to understand better where we've gone awry personally and socially, and to find our collective way back to peace.

This is why, in the Ignatian tradition, we speak of *desiring* the will of God. We want to desire that which is good and just for the entirety of the universe. We want to let go of desires that stand in the way of the good.

"The 'will of God,'" writes Fr. Greg Boyle, SJ, a Jesuit priest who has spent years working with gang members in Los Angeles, California, "is never different from what we most deeply want. Ensuring, then, that we never are strangers to ourselves will give us access to our deepest longings."[55] This is where contemplation and reflection come into play. We need to know ourselves so as to know our desires. In that knowing, we enter into Mystery.

Concepts of nonaction and Zen help me better understand the practice of Ignatian indifference in the spiritual life and the surrender of self to that which is larger. It brings the words of Ignatius of Loyola into sharper focus: "Our one desire and choice should be what is more conducive to the end for which we are created."[56] *Of course* we would want that. We *want* to tap into that greater flow of the universe, find our place in it, and *live* there. It becomes that much easier to understand and embrace Ignatius's First Principle and Foundation: "As far as we are concerned, we should not prefer health to sickness, riches to poverty, honor to dishonor, a long life to a short life."[57] We simply want to *be* who we *are* right *now*.

The desire, then, to put ourselves at the disposal of this force, known by some as the will of God, comes into clarity. Ignatius ends the *Spiritual Exercises* by inviting retreatants to pray the *Suscipe* Prayer: "Take, Lord, and receive all my liberty, my memory, my understanding and my entire will, all that I have and possess. . . . Dispose of it wholly according to your will."[58] Essentially, we pray to live a life of nonaction so that we simply *are* in the great flow of the universe.

THE JEDI CODE

One of the movie posters commissioned to promote *Episode II: Attack of the Clones* shows Hayden Christensen as Anakin Skywalker standing back-to-back with Natalie Portman's Padmé Amidala. The text above them reads, "A Jedi shall not know anger. Nor hatred. Nor love." The scene is lit by the glow of a red lightsaber.

These words paraphrase the Jedi Code, which appears in various forms across the franchise but always, at its root, points to a need to practice detachment: *There is no emotion, there is peace. There is no ignorance, there is knowledge. There is no passion, there is serenity. There is no chaos, there is harmony.*[59] The red saber in the *Attack of the Clones* poster hints at the cost of failing to adhere to this teaching. We know, of course, that Anakin *does* become attached—to Padmé and eventually to power—and that this attachment ultimately corrupts him.

Reath Silas, a Jedi Padawan of the High Republic era, sums up what it means to be a Jedi in Claudia Gray's young adult novel *Into the Dark*: "The Jedi are Force users united in our quest to understand the mysteries of the Force and to serve as guardians of peace and justice throughout the galaxy. . . . We ground ourselves in a spiritual existence and give up individual attachments in order to focus entirely on greater concerns."

His counterpart, a young pilot named Affie, retorts, "So, that means no sex." Reath bashfully nods his head in agreement.[60] It's a funny exchange about a serious topic, but it gets to the heart of the matter: detachment from all things as a baseline rule—all the things that make us *human*—isn't healthy.

Another Jedi, Orla Jareni, from the High Republic era—
and from another novel by Claudia Gray, *The Fallen Star*—
provides this insight: "The real danger lies in those emotions
that seem positive at first but take too great a hold over our
minds and hearts. Give way to those feelings, embrace them,
and before you know it, they've been twisted into something
else far more damaging."[61] We practice detachment by holding *all* things *lightly*. We let go of them if and when they steer
us astray or are no longer necessary, but we don't shun them
out of hand. We never allow anything to hold inordinate control over us. This is Ignatian indifference.

Unfortunately, this nuanced approach is not what a
young Anakin Skywalker learns. And he's corrupted by
Palpatine as a result. Recall Yoda's advice—unheeded though
it was—to a flailing Anakin to let go of all those things he
feared to lose. Rather than let go, Anakin sought control.

The Jedi, though, were no perfect practitioners of
detachment. In Delilah S. Dawson's novel *Inquisitor: Rise
of the Red Blade*, a young Jedi, Iskat Akaris, seeks answers
about her own past. But Jedi librarian Jocasta Nu discourages
Iskat's inquiries. "Attachment is forbidden," Jocasta says.
"That includes attachment to a name, a people, a place." But
does this response help Iskat practice detachment? Of course
not. It demonstrates the Jedi Order's inordinate attachment
to its own rules. And Iskat, who is curious about nothing
less than her own identity, is unable to practice indifference.
Since she is not given the information she seeks, she is unable
to hold it *lightly*. This is the dark side at work. It's no wonder
Iskat finds herself on a dark path."[62]

There's a brilliant bit in the finale of the first season of
Andor where we hear the voice of the fallen rebel, Nemik,

reading aloud from his manifesto. "The Imperial need for control is so desperate because it is so unnatural," he says. "Tyranny requires constant effort. It breaks, it leaks. Authority is brittle. Oppression is the mask of fear."

See how a need for control and fear go hand in hand? What, then, does that say of indifference, a willingness to hold all things lightly and surrender to the cosmic flow of the universe?

"I am one with the Force, and the Force is with me." The mantra of Chirrut Îmwe, but perhaps ours, too. Can we see ourselves surrendering control to a greater power? Or do we cling to control, cling to fragile rules and structures, cling to what we know will inevitably be washed away?

THREE KINDS OF PEOPLE

How do we practice this detachment? Ignatius offers a meditation on three kinds of people. All three desire to conform to the will of God, to live wu wei, to practice Zen. And yet they are still attached to something in their lives: a large sum of money, or prestige and power, a job or a house or a way of living.

And so, the first kind of person *procrastinates*. They know that life could hold so much more, that they are falling short of their potential, and yet they fear letting go. They never do.

The second kind of person *compromises*. They step into the flowing river but never fully surrender to the rushing current. They want to both cling to what they have *and* surrender to the greater needs of the world. They never fully commit.

The third kind of person achieves wu wei by *practicing indifference.* "They seek only to will and not will as God . . . inspires them," Ignatius writes. "They will make efforts neither to want that, nor anything else, unless the service of God . . . moves them to do so. As a result, the desire to be better able to serve . . . will be the cause of their accepting anything or relinquishing it."[63]

This meditation on three hypothetical kinds of people connects naturally to the Two Standards. We meditate on a need to move away from pride, honor, and wealth in favor of humility, rejection, and poverty. In the process, we hold all things lightly so as to discover where we're being pulled. Again, we hear something similar in the path of Zen: "The compassionate actor never asks what he gets from helping," writes Bortolin. "He just sees what needs to be done and does it—selflessly."[64] We cling to nothing (including ourselves) so as to remain aware and available to the needs of the moments, needs that only we, aligned with the flow of the universe, the will of God, can meet—without even realizing it.

CALM, PEACE, PASSIVE—ACTION

Let's return to our droids in the desert. C-3PO isn't wrong: It does often feel as though life is made up of one difficulty after another. We lose loved ones; we're fired from jobs. Our roofs leak, and childcare is expensive, and our cat just threw up all over the carpet. There's racism and sexism and homophobia and a distrust of strangers. Children go to bed hungry, and bombs fall on playgrounds.

Are we made to suffer? It sure can feel that way. And in those feelings of insecurity, doubt, and fear, we make rash decisions. We fear what we can't control, and so we react by seeking control so as to be less afraid. Or we throw up our hands in an act of nihilistic fury. Nothing—not suffering or joy or pain or triumph—seems to matter. Why bother caring?

The path of indifference proposes a third way.

Look to R2. No matter how sandy the planet, how determined the battle droids, or how mysterious the Jedi, R2-D2 trundles onward. The droid does what he is, what he's made to do, persistent even in the highs and lows of galactic living. He's plugged in—literally.

We can be R2-D2. We carry within us inherent goodness, life, and hope. It's only natural that we sometimes get bogged down in the day-to-day, but never so much so that we can't decide today, now, in this very moment, to carry on. We have something within us the galaxy needs. We are someone's—perhaps, a lot of someone's—greatest hope for a better present and future.

And when we realize all of this, when we recognize that we have the power to choose our next step—that next right thing—no matter the chaos all around us, no matter how small the step may seem to be, we discover that we are part of something greater. The whole universe pulses with this divine spark, and we are part of it. We can see it, tap into it, embody it. What will we choose? What decision will bring us closer to that greater good we hope to realize, to justice and peace and beauty and wonder?

Luke asks Yoda how he will know the light from the darkness. How he will know how to choose. Yoda responds that first it is necessary to cultivate a sense of calm, to be at peace, even passive. Only when we have made ourselves indifferent to all that is swirling around us can we decide what should come next. It is then that we can hear the still, quiet voice of God. It is never from a place of desperation and anxiety and fear that good decisions are made. Instead, first we must cultivate indifference. We become the manifestation of the third type of person in Ignatius's meditation.

We seek the light. We look for those decisions that will bring us closer to it. We search for what will empower us to shine our own light out into a world often dominated by shadow. In the meantime, we roll on, across the sandy deserts, aware and mindful of all that is around us, trusting in the hope embedded within us, trusting that if we commit ourselves to its realization, then it will, in fact, be realized. That this, indeed, is *our* mission. And the whole galaxy will be better for it.

WAYFINDER EXERCISE

I AM ONE WITH THE FORCE

1. **Reach out.** Picture in your mind the great flowing nature of the universe, a rushing river of possibility and potential. What does it look like? What colors do you see?

2. **Set your intention.** You desire to find your place within that rushing river. You desire to throw yourself into its flowing energy and discover where it leads—and where, specifically, it leads *you*. But something holds you back.

   Make your mantra by completing this sentence: *I make myself indifferent to . . .* what? *. . . and join the flow of the universe.* Repeat that mantra several times. Be mindful of your breath.

3. **Review the past.** As you repeat your mantra, allow your mind to wander. Where does it go? Are you thinking of a moment from earlier today, earlier this year, or many years ago? Do you see moments where you clearly surrendered yourself to the flowing power of the universe? How did it feel? What did it reveal about your unique self? Do you see moments when you resisted? How did it feel by contrast?

   Settle on a single moment. What insight does this moment reveal to you?

4. **Always in motion.** The moment you've settled on from your past necessarily informs your present and might guide you into the future. Are there invitations now to join in this flow? Does a name for this invitation bubble up within you? Will of God? Dao? Zen? Something else? What feels right for you?

5. **This is the way.** Remember this: Cultivating a disposition of indifference prepares you to make good choices, to act for the good from that place of constant flow. Is there a pending decision in your life that could benefit from such a practice?

End your reflection by cultivating a disposition of gratitude to yourself, the universe, and the infinite Other.

CHAPTER 10

INSTITUTIONS

An article appeared in the *National Catholic Reporter* in the days following the live-action debut of fan-favorite character Ahsoka Tano, in the second season of *The Mandalorian*. The article, written by Jennifer Vosters, was titled "In An Age of Institutional Failure, 'Star Wars' Is Saving My Faith."[65] The themes Vosters explored bounced around in my head for days, forever changing how I view Ahsoka.

Vosters identifies as "a Catholic woman and a diehard science-fiction/fantasy fan." As a result, she says, "I'm used to feeling underrepresented." So for Vosters, Ahsoka's character development in the animated series *The Clone Wars* was a breath of fresh air. Not only is Ahsoka a compelling, three-dimensional Jedi whose hero journey, "blossoming from saber-wielding pipsqueak to steadfast peace-seeker," got the screen time and script attention it deserved, but in the end, Ahsoka's character arc was shocking.

She walked away from the Jedi Order.

She walked away from the only life she'd ever known. And she did so because they—the great, moral, awe-inspiring Jedi—had failed her and failed themselves. They'd allowed themselves to become too cozy with corrupt politicians.

They'd forgotten what it meant to stand with the weak, the forgotten, the outcast. And even when they realized their mistake, even when Ahsoka is proven innocent of the crime for which she was wrongly accused, her Jedi friends' half-hearted apology is not enough to reverse this stinging betrayal.

Ahsoka does not want to be readmitted into this flawed and failing Order. She chooses to chart her own path.

Vosters writes that she "watched in shock as a familiar kind of deconstruction unfolded onscreen: A young woman realizing that the institution she loved did not love her back. That the leaders she trusted failed to preserve the core principles of their creed and would continue, again and again, to ally with the powerful. That she must choose between her faith—her connection to the Divine and to herself—and the very community that taught her."[66]

I remember watching that episode—the finale of *The Clone Wars*' fifth season. I assumed that Ahsoka would find her way back into the Order through a subplot of a subsequent season. Such thinking likely betrays something of my own biases: "Of *course* she'll want back in. What else is she going to do? What else is out there for her? This is the *Jedi Order* we're talking about!"

A lot of well-meaning religious people are tempted to think this same way.

But that's not what happens. It's the Jedi that go all but extinct and Ahsoka who lives on. The institution itself is nearly wiped from the map, but one of its greatest acolytes goes on to embody its best principles.

There's a dance going on here between the individual and the institution. In this chapter, we will reflect upon this dance, leaning on various aspects of the Ignatian tradition we've already seen throughout this book.

SPIRITUAL, RELIGIOUS, OR SOMETHING MORE?

So often we are tempted to place ourselves squarely in one camp: I am *spiritual* but not religious; or you can't possibly be spiritual *without* being religious; or I need no one to tell me how to live my spirituality! Or we believe we must seek out the sacred in community; the individual's experience is secondary. In truth, a community is built upon individuals, and a religion is only as good as the *living* spirituality it nurtures.

Time and again, Ahsoka returns to the Jedi. To the institution it once represented. The institution it might be in the future. She turns to Anakin and Obi-Wan when Maul becomes a renewed threat in the final days of the Clone Wars. She teams up with Kanan and Ezra in *Rebels* on self-described "Jedi business." In *The Mandalorian*, thinking that he might be the start of a new generation of Jedi, she sets Grogu on his path to Luke Skywalker. Ahsoka takes on an (admittedly) nontraditional Padawan of her own in Sabine Wren. And her copilot and travel companion, Huyang, is an ancient droid constructed for the very purpose of preserving the Jedi Order. Clearly, Ahsoka still feels love for the Jedi. Even if she no longer identifies as a Jedi, she loves what the institution at its best represents. She recognizes its importance—dare we say, necessity—to the galaxy. Perhaps she even still has something to learn from its members past, present, and future.

Think about your own past or present relationship with a religious organization or institution. Do you see something of yourself reflected in Ahsoka's journey?

Regardless of the spiritual tradition with which we identify, it's worthwhile to reflect on what we might learn from Ahsoka and from the character that, I will argue, embodies her opposite: Yoda.

ALWAYS MORE TO LEARN THERE IS

No one is more of an institution in the Jedi Order than Yoda. During the time of the High Republic, hundreds of years before the Clone Wars and the Empire, Yoda was already a well-respected, much-admired, very powerful Jedi Master. He had been at this Jedi thing for centuries before he would preside over the Order's downfall.

We catch a glimpse of this institutional blindness in the audio drama *Dooku: Jedi Lost.* Yoda breaks up a duel between his then-apprentice and eventual nemesis, Dooku, and another Jedi. Consumed by worry that his counterpart is a Sith, Dooku has lost control over his emotions.

"Master Yoda. Dooku saw something down there," the other Jedi says, referring to the Jedi archives. "We need to know what it was!" She's worried that the Jedi Order isn't proactively working to prepare the galaxy for a potential return of the Sith.

But Yoda waves her concern away. "What's done is done. Repressed the memory, his mind has. The way he should. The way he has been trained."[67]

The other Jedi presses the point. "What if we're wrong? What if reducing [the Sith] to a footnote of history is playing into their hands?" She suggests training Jedi younglings to identify and combat Sith artifacts. She insists Yoda and the Jedi Council consult the prophecies.

"Unknowable the future is," Yoda counters. "Only to the dark side, prophecy leads. To doubt and fear. An old argument this is."[68]

Yoda dismisses the threat of an eventual Sith uprising; he adheres to the Jedi Code and the path of the light side. And yet, we viewers know that the Sith *do* return, and the galaxy *is* plunged into darkness. If Yoda had been less rigid, more curious, would he have been able to act in time to save the Jedi, to prevent the countless lives lost and ruined in the wake of the Clone Wars and the Galactic Empire?

Are we too rigid? Do we lack curiosity? Are we on a similar trajectory as Master Yoda in our own spiritual lives?

"It is time we inform the Senate that our ability to use the Force has diminished," the great Jedi Master Mace Windu counsels Yoda after the two learn that a clone army has been created without their knowledge—and at the supposed request of a long-dead Jedi, no less!

Yoda is unconvinced, certain that only the Dark Lord of the Sith, whoever that is, knows of the Jedi's weakness. "If informed the Senate is, multiply our adversaries will." And so, even all those years later, in *Attack of the Clones*, Yoda still desires to suppress and conceal failures, mistakes, and weaknesses.

I wonder if we glimpse here the interplay of the Two Standards, and the clear temptation to the enemy's standard, in Yoda's desire to conceal his own tenuous hold on power. Recall again how the evil spirit flourishes in secrecy and shadow.

Is Yoda trying to shore up the cracks that are appearing in the Jedi Order? Is he frustrated with himself for going along with the prophecy surrounding Anakin Skywalker, an act he's already admitted was more in line with the dark side? Is he clinging to the remnants of power and, as it wanes, attempting to masquerade as though he still possesses it?

And do we see any of these characteristics in our own spiritual path, our own religious tradition?

I don't think Yoda-as-institution is so easily vilified. After all, Yoda continues to train the younglings. He continues to counsel his fellow Jedi and serve the Galactic Republic. His actions demonstrate hope in a better, evolving future. Perhaps he got too comfortable. The rug of the galaxy was pulled out from under him. Plus, we shouldn't discount the manipulations of Darth Sidious, the dark side, and the enemy's standard.

We, too, should avoid vilifying ourselves and our communities so quickly. Much good is done the world over in the name of religion, spirituality, and faith. It's perhaps unfortunate that so often it's only bad news that makes the headlines.

BLINDNESS, SIGHT, AND HOPE

We discover in the sixth season of *The Clone Wars* that Yoda knows the Jedi will fall and fail, and that the Clone Wars have been a tool of the dark side from the beginning. In the very cave on Dagobah into which he will usher a young Luke Skywalker more than two decades later, Yoda glimpses the downfall of the Jedi in a vision of the death of his friends. As he emerges from the cave, he hears a voice. It is Qui-Gon Jinn. The long-dead Jedi warns, "Dark times are ahead. Forces of light must remain."

Yoda is ready to give up hope. "There is always hope, my friend," Qui-Gon counters. "Though it often comes in forms not looked for. The key is knowing how to see it."[69]

I think this charge—this ever-present Star Wars theme of hope found in surprising places—is what ultimately takes Yoda from powerful Jedi Master sitting atop the temple on Coruscant to exiled hermit living in the swamps of Dagobah. Hope grows where we least expect it.

How might a commitment to seek out hope in forms not often looked for change our spiritual lives? Might such a commitment keep us engaged, even when we see so clearly the failures and shortcomings? Might such a commitment help us emerge from our own caves, even when all seems lost?

"Your arrogance blinds you," Darth Sidious says when confronted with Yoda's last-ditch effort to defeat the Sith. I think Yoda knows that Sidious is right.

Having fallen from that place of pride, Yoda switches from one Standard to the other when he embraces rejection and humility. The institution he served for centuries failed, its own shortcoming a reflection of Yoda's. And so, Yoda walks a different path, a different way of the Force, that of a recluse, lost to reflection and contemplation. Who more aptly embodies rejection than a failed Jedi passing time in a swamp?

But, taking Qui-Gon's words to heart, Yoda does his part to ensure that the light remains. Perhaps embracing a path of humility and rejection makes us more able to shine clearly the light we have buried within.

FAILURE: OUR GREATEST TEACHER

I am struck by this depiction of Yoda as a Jedi who knew that what he loved, what he had worked for, and what he'd spent centuries of life representing was doomed to failure. He *saw* it. He no doubt saw his own complicity, his own personal failures. And yet, he didn't give up. He didn't surrender the war or hang up his lightsaber. He kept going. He kept going even *after* it was all over, even *after* he found himself on Dagobah. He trained more Jedi. He believed in a better future beyond his own failures.

Was his path better, worse, or just different from Ahsoka's?

I've spent the majority of my professional life employed by the Catholic Church. For much of that time, I've worked in communications. In many ways, I represent the institution, even when things are said and done that break my heart, make me angry and sorrowful, and make me want to bury my head somewhere. I'm tied up in it. I think of the great suffering the Catholic Church has caused Indigenous communities, members of the LGBTQ+ community, victims of sexual abuse, and so many more. What can I do but feel sorrow and shame, and wonder why I continue associating with such an organization?

At the same time, the Catholic Church does tremendous good, and I've seen and experienced that firsthand, too. I've accompanied colleagues at Catholic Relief Services to remote regions of the world where young people are being educated, fed, and empowered to dream thanks to the dedicated work of the Catholic Church and its partners. I've volunteered at soup kitchens staffed by Catholic Charities, feeding and housing those who are down on their luck and in need of a boost to get to the next chapter of their story. Jesuit priests, Carmelite sisters, and sisters of Bon Secours help me imagine a *new* way of being Church: one that is inclusive and joyful and brimming with hope. I've experienced the power and wisdom of the spiritual traditions within the Catholic faith; my own spiritual life is a testament to this wisdom that has come before me. And Pope Francis, the man himself, has inspired countless Catholics and non-Catholics alike through his leadership and his concern for and commitment to those most in need. These are legacies made possible only by a religious institution.

Many years ago, my then-girlfriend (now-wife) and two friends from college traveled to Montreal, Canada. We stayed at a hostel where we met two young women with whom we were sharing the room. I forget exactly what the conversation consisted of, but something about this awkward sleeping situation inspired one of our new friends to remark that only "enormously religious" people would have a problem with it.

We still laugh at the phrase today. Were they imagining obese monks? No. They meant people who take faith and religion and spirituality seriously. Little did those women know that they were in the company of such people! And yet, how sad if the spiritual life is reduced to legalistic edicts on who can share a hostel room with whom.

If that's all enormously religious people amount to, it's no wonder religious institutions are so often dismissed.

Rather, I think of the words my friend Fr. Jim Mayzik, SJ, shared with me while I was an undergraduate student at Fairfield University. He described religion and the various institutions it creates as "tools to get us near the fire." The fire, of course, is God, the Divine, the Other, the Living Force, that which is ineffable. The institution can get us only so far; we must make that final leap on our own. And it will singe and scorch and burn; fire is not comfortable. Spiritual growth and discovery and deep knowing aren't easy things. But my Jesuit friend was not shy in noting that religious institutions that *fail* to get us nearer to the fire, that keep us *comfortable* with the status quo, are not, in fact, doing what they are meant to do. As Yoda might say: Those, leave behind, we can.

FIRST, ORDER—BUT ALWAYS CHANGE

"Some people are grateful for order, just begging for rules to follow."[70] This from Archex, formerly known as Captain Cardinal, a high-ranking, red-armored stormtrooper of the First Order. The Resistance spy, Vi Moradi, helped him to see the evil he was perpetrating, helped him glimpse the oppressive systems he was creating. Even so, working against his former employer is no easy task.

In Delilah S. Dawson's Star Wars novel *Galaxy's Edge: Black Spire*, we see Archex beginning to grasp how the First Order imposed and held power, and what that means for him now. "You'd see them exhale in relief [those who were grateful for order] when they saw our uniforms and then glare smugly at their troublesome neighbors, feeling that they themselves were safe because they were righteous."[71]

The First Order are the villains, representing a resurgence of imposed order across the galaxy. Whose order? To what end? What voices are left out of the order-making? These are all questions worth asking, as General Leia Organa and her Resistance soldiers do.

We the viewers—or, in this case, the readers—might take these supposed bad guys on face value. They're the villains, and that's that. But the idea of order—of making some discernible sense of the seeming chaos all around us—isn't inherently an evil thing. It's what religions do; it's in large part what our spiritual quests consist of. How do we organize our lives—our *understanding* of our lives—in a way that makes meaning?

Doesn't this necessitate some sort of order?

That orderly way of proceeding down a tried-and-true path, following wise leaders to whom we might turn and listen, adopting practices and traditions that help us build on what's come before is, likely, something we all seek. It's something glimpsed, for better and worse, in religions the world over.

But context matters, right? Those questions—*Whose order? For whom and for what? How does order evolve and improve?*—matter. Order that is not interrogated, reflected upon, and brought into dialogue with lived experience can become oppressive and destructive.

So look back at Captain Cardinal's words and ask yourself: Am *I* grateful for order? Why? Because there are a few ways to go from here. We might be grateful for order in our lives because it helps us make sense and make meaning and then, importantly, take that next courageous step closer to the fire, as my Jesuit friend advised.

We do not uphold order for its own sake; we uphold order in so far as it helps all of us and all of the created world to improve, to grow, to come closer to who and what we are meant to be. To encounter the living God. To do anything less is to make a god of the very *idea* of order—and what a sad god that is.

The other temptation that we see in Captain Cardinal's words is the temptation to self-righteousness. The temptation to use our order—be it religion, race, socioeconomic status, what have you—to create an *us* and a *them*. We act as though by blindly following the rules of this new order, we are better than others, set apart, saved.

If we were really close to the fire, we'd know that those "troublesome neighbors" are just as essential to the endgame of the spiritual life as we are. As Pope Francis reminds us: "No one is saved alone; we can only be saved together."[72]

THE IGNATIAN PARADOX

Ironically, Ignatius of Loyola ran afoul of the Spanish Inquisition on more than one occasion. The institutional Catholic Church of his time did not trust his approach, this idea that we could know the will of God and act on it simply through our own prayer and contemplation. Ignatius is very clear that the Creator deals directly with the creature, and that any spiritual director should get out of the way of God speaking directly to the individual.

What's the problem for the institutional Catholic Church? Well, if God is unknowable, then who can say what this ineffable Creator will communicate to us individuals?

At the same time, in "Rules for Thinking with the Church," Ignatius holds that, right out of the gate, "we must put aside all judgment of our own, and keep the mind ever ready and prompt to obey in all things . . . the Church."[73] Confusing? Perhaps. Or is this an invitation to a creative tension, a spiritual paradox that is not uncommon across all religious traditions? We allow ourselves to be challenged by, and offer a challenge to, the institutions that have formed us. We learn, listen, grow, and adapt.

Our spiritual journey is ripe with opportunities to encounter the sacred and then bring that encounter into dialogue with the experiences of others. We pull and tug, and in it all we glimpse something of the spiritual depth of creation. We discount no one; we do not silence the Spirit as it blows across the universe in new ways. Building on the past, we respond to the needs of the moment. We make amends for mistakes made while not letting past failure dictate the future.

We need both the willingness to seek out something new, to be a seeker, to embrace the seekers among us, *and* we need the institution, the storehouse of knowledge and tradition, the community that learns and grows and fails and muddles onward with each new passing generation.

THE SEEKER AND MASTER

Claudia Gray's High Republic novel *The Fallen Star* offers an illustrative exchange between Wayseeker Orla Jareni, a Jedi who has decided to embrace a path apart from that dictated by the Jedi Order, and Jedi Master and Council Member Stellan Gios.

"You've never felt free to search, or to fail," Orla accuses Stellan. "You've never had the luxury to chart your own path. Is that why you're threatened by the Wayseekers who do?"

Stellan replies, "I'm not threatened. And we're meant to follow the path the Order and the Force show us."

"That's where we differ," Orla retorts. "You still think the Jedi Order and the Force are the same thing."[74]

Whatever we call God is and always will be beyond the grasp—beyond the *knowing*—of any religious institution. We must not let that discourage us from setting out on our own spiritual path, from deepening our engagement with our own tradition. And we cannot let that cause us to distrust those whose paths and traditions differ from ours.

There's a brief moment in *Star Wars Rebels* when Ahsoka and Yoda meet again. Yoda is not *really* in the crumbling temple; it's a projection, a vision of sorts. But he's real enough. So when he locks eyes with Ahsoka as she and two fugitive Jedi, Kanan Jarrus and Ezra Bridger, are fleeing for their lives, she glances back just long enough to see her old mentor. He inclines his head ever so slightly and gives her a nod of approval. Gratitude, too, I think, for the part she is playing.

Ahsoka smiles back.

The individual, and the institution. The seeker, and the tradition. One acting as guide, the other as knowledge. Both recognizing the essential value of the other for the good of the whole.

A LEGACY OF FAILURE—AND POSSIBILITY

In *The Last Jedi*, an old and jaded Luke Skywalker angrily dismisses the institution of the Jedi Order. He believes they've become romanticized. He insists that once you strip all the legend and story away, "the legacy of the Jedi is failure." He points to none other than the creation and rise of his own father, Darth Vader, at the hands of the Jedi themselves to prove the point.

He's not wrong. And yet, Rey still seeks out the Jedi. The true seeker looks to the tradition not to get cozy with the powerful but to make sense of and build upon what's come before, what those grappling with the mysteries of the galaxy have learned and lost. To surround herself with a legion of saints and sinners who have already walked the long, difficult road of the Living Force.

Luke is an unwilling teacher; he drives Rey away. It is Yoda as a Force ghost who shows up to set Luke straight. In a powerful scene, the little green master underscores the importance of the tradition that religious institutions nourish, even as they also embrace the need for the individual seeker to go beyond the institution itself.

"Pass on what you have learned," Yoda says. "Failure, most of all. The greatest teacher, failure is. We are what they grow beyond. That is the true burden of all masters."

WHAT WE GROW BEYOND

1. **Reach out.** Imagine your own spiritual community—however you define such a thing. Who is part of it? Where do you gather? What do you do together? What feelings does this group evoke in you?

2. **Set your intention.** It is necessary to *grow beyond* any and all spiritual communities so as to come closer to and enter into Mystery.

   Make your mantra by completing this sentence: *I reach beyond by* . . . what? Repeat that mantra several times. Be mindful of your breath.

3. **Review the past.** As you repeat your mantra, allow your mind to wander. Where does it go? Are you thinking of a moment from earlier today, earlier this year, or many years ago? What memories or feelings bubble up when you reflect on your relationship with religious and spiritual institutions—past and present? Where have you found nourishment and encouragement? Where have you found hurt

or wanting? How have these moments formed you into the person you are today?

Settle on a single moment. What insight does this moment reveal to you?

4. **Always in motion.** The moment you've settled on from your past necessarily informs your present and might guide you into the future. Are you being invited to return to a spiritual community or religious institution to discover some new knowledge or wisdom? Are you being invited to seek beyond your own tradition to uncover something yet unknown to you about the world? Or are you simply where you need to be?

5. **This is the way.** Integral to religious institutions is the ebb and flow of community. Who are you being invited to accompany in their own encounter with spiritual community and beyond?

End your reflection by cultivating a disposition of gratitude to yourself, the universe, and the infinite Other.

CHAPTER 11

REDEMPTION

In the premiere episode of the third season of *The Mandalorian*, our titular hero, Din Djarin, is in search of redemption. He has removed his helmet—seemingly the worst thing a member of his Mandalorian sect, the Children of the Watch, can do—and has been cast out of his clan. His supposed sin is weighing on him, and he's determined to make things right.

In that first episode, we immediately see two divergent opinions on the matter. The leader of Mando's clan, the Armorer, has all but written him off. She's the one who has declared him an apostate, and she doesn't believe he'll be able to redeem himself. After all, she says, any hope of redemption lies in the living waters in the mines of Mandalore, and that planet has long been destroyed—some even say cursed! All the same, Din is determined to try.

Bo-Katan Kryze, once a member of another Mandalorian sect, Death Watch, merely rolls her eyes at Din's quest and his preoccupation with redemption, helmet wearing, and the Children of the Watch. She assures him that there's nothing magical about the water on Mandalore. (And there's *definitely* nothing living in its depths.) He's wasting his time.

These two takes on redemption are helpful as we begin this chapter. On the one hand, there *is* nothing magical about it. We live lives reflective of our own worth and dignity. Do we allow ourselves to be handicapped by shame, failure, and old wounds? Or do we live in such a way that we atone for past missteps, living reconciliation and building a future of justice? Even in that first episode, we see Din saving his fellow Mandalorians, caring for Grogu, and concerned for the well-being of his friends. To us, the viewers, Din *is* a Mandalorian; he proves himself worthy of that title again and again.

On the other hand, ritual is important. It is the outward manifestation of internal truths. It is the *doing* of spirituality; it is the invitation to continual self-reflection. It's not so much the magical thinking as it is the clear and constant action of self-improvement for the good of all.

St. Ignatius, in his own spiritual practices, invites us to consider demonstrating love through action, not mere words. Ritual was important to him as a demonstration of that constant activity. But ritual, too, can be reduced to mere words that remove the heart of any real-world significance. Redemption requires both.

REDEEMED VILLAINS

Star Wars offers us an important lesson in seeing—doggedly seeking, even—the good in people who seem made of nothing but pure evil.

Count Dooku, tragic in his own way, is a man who made too many wrong choices (albeit for the right reasons). There are those who try to save him because they believe he can turn back. In *Tales of the Jedi*, we watch as Master Yaddle goes to her death believing Count Dooku can be redeemed. Qui-Gon Jinn is another one who seems to have died never having written his old master off. Both Qui-Gon and Yaddle cling to their hope, allowing it to guide their actions toward the treatment of others. They understand Dooku's desire to bring justice to the galaxy, even if they can't justify his actions.

This sense of insistent hope, though, is most apparent in the stories of Darth Vader and Kylo Ren. The redemptive character arc almost feels like a Star Wars trope—*of course* they're going to come back to the light. They *have* to. We can't leave Anakin or Ben in darkness!

And so it goes: Luke Skywalker manages to break through to his father at the last moment, and Vader saves his son by destroying their common enemy. Ben Solo's return to the light is buttressed by the sacrifice of his father, Han Solo, the confidence of his counterpart, Rey, and the Force-defying willpower of his mother, Leia Organa. He, too, rediscovers the light and returns to Exegol in time to stand against Palpatine.

Both Anakin and Ben have their conversion moments, those realizations that they *can* still put aside the darkness of their past, terrible as their deeds may have been, and come back to what is good and just. We return to that Ignatian concept of a cannonball moment: Anakin and Ben are certainly knocked off their feet and thrown from their current trajectory before being given a chance to chart a new path. The outstretched hands of Luke and Rey represent the invitation of persistent hope that redemption is always possible— redemption meaning a turning back and a recommitment to what is good and right.

Both men die on the side of right, heroes if only to those who witnessed their final moments. Redemption is redemption, no matter who is or isn't around to see it.

A HERO REDEEMED IN THE WOODS WITH NO ONE AROUND TO SEE IT . . .

And yet. A true conversion—a true cannonball moment—demands an ongoing, sustained response. Our actions are the outward manifestation of our beliefs and values. (That's where Count Dooku got it wrong, what with all the killing, warmongering, and deception. His values and actions were not aligned.) The opportunity to continue to act upon them, to demonstrate—slowly, haltingly, perhaps even inconsistently—that we are trying to live this new way of life is important. That's part of ritual, and why rituals are something we do repeatedly.

Anakin and Ben never receive opportunities to demonstrate ongoing commitment. They have their moment of conversion; they return to the light. They act for the good of the galaxy. But then they die as a result. A noble sacrifice, yes, but a sudden ending to any further opportunities to live out that redemption.

It's not so much the fate of their eternal souls I'm concerned about; both men became one with the Force. But it would have made for an interesting story to see how Anakin and Ben worked to reenter galactic society. How do monsters shed their monstrous skin and regain their humanness? Just as important, questions must be asked: Do *we*, the citizens of this supposed galactic society, *allow* them to? How *do* flawed individuals demonstrate their commitment to change? How do they demonstrate their sorrow for past failings? How does society welcome them back? These, too, are questions of hope.

At the Battle of Crait in *The Last Jedi*, a nearly defeated General Leia Organa says to her Jedi brother that she had held out hope that her son would return to the light. But now she admits that he is gone. Luke, perhaps recognizing his own past misconceptions and mistakes, surprises her when he says, "No one's ever really gone."

That's where hope meets redemption, not just in our personal spiritual lives but in the communities of which we are a part. We have to continue to hope and make room for redemption, even in the face of the failings and shame of ourselves and others. It's never too late. No one—not us, not those we love, or those we purport to disdain—is ever really too far gone.

THE NECESSARY WORKING-OUT OF REDEMPTION

Anakin and Ben don't get the chance to demonstrate their commitment to a changed way of life. For most of the galaxy, it doesn't really matter. Evil has been toppled.

In the case of Vader, he's banished to the history books. In Claudia Gray's Leia-focused novel, *Bloodline*, we learn that, to the next generation of New Republic citizens, "Vader had seemed almost like some folktale creature from stories told to frighten little children so they wouldn't run away from home."[75] Anakin's name was never cleared; he was never redeemed in the public eye. And Leia, "the child of a figure so widely hated as Darth Vader," soon found her own reputation imperiled when her heritage became thrust into the center of galactic politics.[76]

I would suggest what Star Wars teaches us about redemption is twofold: We must hold out hope for the goodness in others and ourselves, giving space and encouragement to find the light within and return to it. This is what Luke, Rey, Leia, and Han did for Anakin and Ben. It's what we can do for ourselves—reminding ourselves always of our inner, original goodness, and the ongoing opportunity to return to it. It's what we can do for others. We make space for hope.

But the second piece is equally important: We must do the hard work of grappling with the implications of that redemption. We must learn from and act upon our own cannonball moments. It's tempting to think of these conversions—these turnings-back-to-the-light—as one and done. Too many religious folks see conversion in this way. But in fact, the real work begins after the cannonball strike, as we mend our wounds and set out to make right both our internal and external missteps and create a new way of living.

This is not to say that we must always—or even *can* always—be perfect in the wake of this sort of redemption. Certainly not. Anakin and Ben had it easy, from a certain point of view: one final act of ultimate self-sacrificial goodness and then, end scene. The working out of redemption, the living into what a new way of being means, is much harder. It demands reconciliation with self and with others. We must right our relationships, atone for our sins, and pledge to do better in the future.

We see that in the heroes of the Rebellion. We see it clearly in *Andor*.[77] These are imperfect people trying to muddle through an imperfect world, all the while creating something worth living and dying for. Cassian is the titular hero, but he sure does a lot of morally questionable things. He kills folks in cold blood. He abandons friends and family. He works not for the cause but for money. And yet slowly,

slowly, he finds his way closer and closer to becoming the rebel hero who makes the ultimate sacrifice on the sandy beaches of Scarif in *Rogue One*.[78]

Andor doesn't start out perfect. And he makes plenty of mistakes. But he's determined to keep struggling, to keep working out a redemptive arc in his own life for the good of others.

"We've all done terrible things on behalf of the Rebellion," he admits in *Rogue One*. It doesn't sit well with him. But even in moments of darkness, he tries to glimpse the light, the reason he's struggling onward, that ultimate destination. He has to connect his actions to his values, to his beliefs, to his *why*. That's what gets him in that U-wing and on a fatal course for Scarif. Mistakes get made. But if we allow them to define us, to be the final entry in our story, then we truly have failed.

This is why the Two Standards are so important to the spiritual life. They help guide us as we stumble down the many paths in our lives. They help us discern the spirits as we struggle to keep hope and goodness at the forefront of all we do while we muddle ahead toward the light. We keep getting back up, hopeful that we can right whatever wrongs we see in ourselves and in our world.

It can all be redeemed.

SAVE WHAT YOU LOVE

At the end of the *Spiritual Exercises*, we're invited to reflect on the *contemplatio*, or the Contemplation to Attain Divine Love. This essential step "is the culmination of the weeks of prayer that precede it," writes Fr. Kevin O'Brien, SJ, in his much-loved book on the Exercises, *The Ignatian Adventure*. In many ways, the Contemplation draws on that commitment to indifference—to put ourselves at the service of the Holy Spirit at work in the universe—and then gives a specific direction to that desire. "We see that the whole movement of the [Spiritual Exercises] retreat has been rooted in and oriented toward love," Fr. O'Brien says.[79]

So what do we do with that knowledge? Ignatius writes, "Love ought to manifest itself in deeds rather than in words . . . [and] love consists in a mutual sharing of goods."[80] The entirety of Ignatian spirituality, then, is pointing us into deeper engagement with the world; it is that working-out of redemption that we've been reflecting on throughout this chapter. We experience our own cannonball moment so that we can then go deeper into the needs of our community to heal, reconcile, and love.

Rose Tico says it best in *The Last Jedi* when she reminds us that it's not about "fighting what we hate, but saving what we love."

Saving what we love.

Spirituality made manifest.

Hope that points to something greater.

In the words of the great liberation theologian Gustavo Gutiérrez, "If humanity, each person, is the living temple of God, we meet God in our encounter with others; we encounter God in the commitment to the historical process of humankind."[81]

In short, we're all in this together. History is just the playing field for our communal redemption. God meets us here and is at work here. That's who Jesus is—God's literal entering into history, playing on the same field as all of creation, daring to labor for hope even in moments bereft of its glimmer. Let's make room, then, in our lives for hope—hope in one another, hope in a better world. And then let's act on that hope—right here, right now.

No One's Ever Really Gone

1. **Reach out.** Think of someone who has recently offended you in some way. Hold an image of them in your mind. What feelings does that image evoke? What new feelings bubble up when you recall that even this person is brimming with goodness?

2. **Set your intention.** Redemption requires two things: making space for forgiveness (holding out hope) and doing the work of reconciliation (righting relationships). What do you need to do for yourself or others?

   Make your mantra by completing this sentence: *I am never too far gone, and neither is . . .* who? Repeat that mantra several times. Be mindful of your breath.

3. **Review the past.** As you repeat your mantra, allow your mind to wander. Where does it go? Are you thinking of a moment from earlier today, earlier this year, or many years ago? Do memories surface that make you feel unredeemable? Do faces come to mind of people *you* consider unredeemable? In both cases, inherent goodness lingers; it never abandons us. But can we see it?

   Settle on a single moment. What insight does this moment reveal to you?

4. **Always in motion.** The moment you've settled on from your past necessarily informs your present and might guide you into the future. Too often, our feelings toward the redeemability of others is a reflection of whether we consider ourselves worthy of redemption. Consider what needs changing in your attitude toward the goodness within yourself and within even the seemingly worst person you know.

5. **This is the way.** Redemption is an ongoing activity. We continue to do the hard work of engaging with all that is good and bad within ourselves and our world. Where does this work direct your attention now?

End your reflection by cultivating a disposition of gratitude to yourself, the universe, and the infinite Other.

CHAPTER 12

PILGRIMAGE

Let me tell you a story. Once upon a time in the Basque Country of Spain, there was a shepherd wandering the hillside. As young Rodrigo de Balanzategui tended his flock, he heard the tolling of a bell. *Bing-bong. Bing-bong.*[82]

"A cowbell," he muttered, and wandered from his path in the Aizkorri mountain range to find its source.

He expected to find an animal but instead discovered something peculiar: a small statue of the Blessed Virgin Mary. There it sat, entangled in a thornbush, and next to it was the offending bell. "Arantzan zu?" Rodrigo exclaimed, inadvertently giving the place and the statue its name ("You, among the thorns?").

Our Lady of Arantzazu, known also as Our Lady of the Thorns, depicts Mary with the infant Jesus on her lap, an image traditionally known as Mary, Seat of Wisdom. The statue, discovered in 1468, quickly became a pilgrimage site and the pride of the local people of Gipuzkoa. A shrine was erected around the statue, and the statue itself remained— and remains—on the very spot upon which it was discovered. The shrine would change hands and change shape and size, growing ever bigger, ever more prominent on that mountain-side, but the same small statue would persist.

The intercessory prayers of pilgrims to Our Lady of Arantzazu are credited with bringing a temporary peace to that region of Spain and, as a result, Arantzazu's renown grew, attracting another pilgrim some fifty years after its discovery. That pilgrim was Ignatius of Loyola.

Ignatius had just begun his own journey. He had left his home in Loyola, wondering what this new post-cannonball life would lead to. He spent a single night's vigil before the Lady of Arantzazu in the company of his brother, and then set off for Montserrat, where he would lay down his sword and surrender the last vestige of his former courtly life.

For Ignatius, Arantzazu proved to be a place of grace and strength.

FAIRY TALES ARE MORE THAN TRUE

It all sounds like a fairy tale, right? Something you roll your eyes at and go, "Oh, *really*? A shepherd, a cowbell, and regional peace? Sure."

I admit, that's what I did. I had missed the reference to Arantzazu in Ignatius's autobiography—it's barely a full sentence—and so was quite surprised when my own pilgrim tour bus pulled up the mountainside to the Franciscan Sanctuary of Our Lady of Arantzazu in Oñati.

But as I would soon discover, Arantzazu is not only a foundational moment in Ignatius's pilgrimage. It's an important site for the local Basque community in the present, too. It became one of my favorite stops on our pilgrimage.

Arantzazu is a place of beauty. Soft fog rolls over the deeply forested mountains, making it feel like a fairy tale.

The sanctuary, where this tiny, ancient statue is elevated high above those who gather, is dark, quiet, and somber. It is a place where people can reflect on internal as well as external conflict.

But the lesson of Arantzazu isn't theological or literary; it's profoundly spiritual. It points to the very meaning of pilgrimage: pilgrims may set off with a destination in mind, but the true purpose of pilgrimage is to be awake, alert, and available to the Holy hidden in the proverbial thorn bushes. It requires not a small amount of practiced indifference. And you don't even have to travel to Spain.

As we near the end of this book-long pilgrimage, are we mindful of hidden places in our own journeys in which we're invited to encounter something sacred? Do we listen for the clanging of cowbells? Or do we throw up our hands and say, "Whatever. It's all just a fairy tale anyway."

FANDOM AS PILGRIMAGE

At this point, you're likely thinking, *Sure. I understand what a pilgrimage is. But what's it got to do with Star Wars?*

Fair enough.

Star Wars fandom is something like a pilgrimage. We enter into the story at different moments: Some of us experienced the original film in theaters in 1977, the very first foray into a galaxy far, far away. Others of us waited in long lines to be among the first to view the franchise's big screen return in 1999. A whole generation grew up watching animated stories: *The Clone Wars, Rebels,* and *Resistance.* The sequel trilogy in so many ways was a circling back to what was familiar while at the same it charted new territory. Projects like *Star Wars: Visions* and anything LEGO Star Wars gave space for playful, creative, thought-provoking, and boundary-pushing reinterpretations of an old story. And now, with so many new stories being told across television shows, comic books, video games, theme parks, and more, we have the opportunity to return to well-traveled places—hello there, again, Tatooine—and explore unknown regions, entirely new galaxies, and even wander into worlds between worlds.

All that to say: Even though we all walk deeper and deeper into this shared world—this shared experience—of Star Wars, we discover different things at different times. We are drawn to different characters, different stories, different themes. And we are free to come and go as we please. Some of us plunge into every comic book available. Others are content to watch the live-action television shows. We take what we need from the story as we need it.

And that's all just fine. The question is: How can we nurture this disposition of pilgrimage as we travel our own path through that most beloved of galaxies?

PILGRIM: A COMPLICATED PROFESSION

Here's one answer: consider *The Mandalorian*.

Jon Favreau, creator and screenwriter for *The Mandalorian*, shares his perspective. "As somebody who grew up with *Star Wars*, and really having been formed around what I experienced when I was little with the first film, there was some aesthetic to it that I think that I really loved. . . . Nothing [live-action] had been on TV other than the *Holiday Special* and the idea of us telling the story in just a few hours over several years opens us up to this novelization of story."[83]

The old and the new. What was and what might yet be. A journey that began a long time ago but still has many new paths unfolding.

The Mandalorian harkened back to the wild west feel of the original films. It introduced us to a novel character who still felt at home in all that we knew to have come before. The world was beaten up and grungy but still there was hope.

And there was Grogu, known in my household and likely many others as Baby Yoda. There, too, we glimpse the road behind us while charting unknown and exciting new territory ahead. (Baby Yoda necessarily reminds us of the original green Jedi himself even as it forces us to wonder: What's this *new* character's story?) The entire experience of *The Mandalorian* is an invitation to ground ourselves in the wider world, the mythos of Star Wars past and present, while ushering in something new and fresh.

Isn't that what pilgrimage is? We recognize all that has come before—the many feet that have trod this path—and reverence that past. But at the same time we set off on a necessarily unique future. And all along the way, we bask in what we encounter, what we experience, who we have the privilege to meet. The destination will come, but we're still on the road.

EVER-EVOLVING DESTINATIONS

The story of Din Djarin provides us with some spiritual tools with which any good pilgrim is equipped. Mando himself is something of a pilgrim. Traveling the galaxy, his ultimate destination is often foggy, but his focus on the present is absolute. (Bounty hunting, we're assured, tends to be a complicated profession; best to keep your focus on the here and now.)

For much of his life, Mando's bounty hunting was what allowed him to support his clan of fellow Mandalorians and slowly upgrade his beskar armor. That's a spiritual journey in and of itself: finding your way in the galaxy so as to both protect your community (the Mandalorians) and more fully manifest your own tradition and beliefs (the beskar armor). But when he encounters Grogu, everything changes. His current purpose comes into sharper focus, and he gives up some of his old ways so as to protect this new and vulnerable member of his chosen family.

So: an old way of life that isn't bad but could be better, and a sudden, chance encounter that invites a deeper, more meaningful engagement with reality. Mando's story bears resemblance to Ignatius of Loyola in that way. The man's courtly life was turned upside down as soon as that cannonball shattered his leg—but, in truth, Mando's story likely also bears a great deal of resemblance to your story and mine.

What in our past might we learn from and then set aside as we take the next steps on our pilgrimage? How are we being invited to reorient ourselves?

THE PROMISE OF DIALOGUE

What more can we learn from Mando for our own pilgrimages? I suggest three things: first, to nurture our own inner dialogue; second, to engage in outward dialogue with those we meet; and third, to allow the Mystery of the universe time to dialogue with the mystery within us.

INNER DIALOGUE

Foundational to the story of Din Djarin is his Mandalorian identity. It's what gave him purpose after his near-fatal escape from the wreckage of the Clone Wars. Mandalorians rescued him. As a result, he adopted their way of living. That meant never removing your helmet. Mandalorian armor is a sacred thing to all Mandalorians, but to the Children of the Watch this religiosity took on a new level: to *be* Mandalorian meant *never* removing your helmet. This is the way. Din seems to accept that with little trouble; after all, the Mandalorians he had known all seem to have been members of the Watch. He's rooted in that tradition, and it has served him well.

But then Grogu enters his life and takes him on a new path. He finds himself moved by this little creature, this child. He finds himself doing things he never thought he would. He leans into his Mandalorian training, background, expertise—but he does so in a new way, for a new purpose. In the end, he has to decide if there is room in that Mandalorian identity for this child who has found his way into Din's life. That inner dialogue—that grappling with self-purpose and self-identity—is most clearly manifested in Din's decision to remove his helmet and look upon Grogu with unfettered eyes.

Does he give up his identity? The Armorer certainly said so. But is he better for having evolved, for having rooted himself in his tradition while allowing that tradition to grow and make room for others? I think the answer is clear. Personal growth enables him to pass on his tradition to his adopted child.

What masks and helmets do we need to remove? How might we further enrich our own traditions and identity while allowing them to grow? After all, Din did not abandon what came before; he allowed it to unfurl in new ways. And part of that meant *returning* to the very same tradition—to Mandalore and its people. But he didn't stay there. It didn't solely define him.

DIALOGUE WITH OTHERS

Second, let's look at engaging in outward dialogue. Mando is skeptical of the galaxy. Who can blame him? His family was killed, his people were scattered, and the world he claims as his home was long abandoned. He makes a living hunting people. Cynicism and distrust seem par for the course.

But he does operate under the assumptions that true Mandalorians are good and can be trusted. He spends a great deal of time trying to find his people, people he can rely on, people who share a creed. And so, in the first half of season 2, when he stumbles upon a handful of Mandalorians on the watery moon of Trask, he's relieved. *These* are his people. That's why he's so shocked when Bo-Katan and her fellow Mandalorians remove their helmets. He reacts by condemning them.

It takes a bit of convincing before Din comes around, but we can see how this outward dialogue necessarily connects with the inner. Mando needs to meet different people, new people. And have his assumptions challenged. He has to learn that just because folks look like him doesn't mean their life experiences, beliefs, and expectations are the same. He has to expand his circle.

Likewise, Grogu takes Mando into the heart of the Jedi—a historic enemy of the Mandalorians. Fennec Shand is a bounty hunter commissioned to kill Din Djarin—but then she becomes a trusted ally. Assumptions crumble under the weight of experience. So, too, are pilgrimages built on experiences, on chance encounters, and on an openness to learn from and with our fellow pilgrims.

What's more, Din is constantly glimpsing seemingly magical occurrences as Grogu learns how to use the Force. Din knew nothing of the Jedi; how shocking these powers must seem! Straight out of a fairy tale. And yet, Din does not abandon his little friend; he does not steer him solely along the path of the Mandalorian and away from this path of mystery. Mando intentionally brings Grogu to Luke Skywalker. He never stops making himself available; he never refuses to welcome Grogu back. He doesn't force his ways, nor does he abandon them. He can be fully Mandalorian while allowing someone else to be decidedly something different.

He may not have completely understood what was taking place in his midst, but he didn't let that stop him from continuing along the path.

DIALOGUE WITH MYSTERY

Inner dialogue. Outward dialogue. And now, finally, dialogue with mystery. This sounds more exciting in theory than it may turn out to be in practice.

The Mandalorian is full of these moments. Din walks through ice caves in the company of the Frog Lady in search of a fix for a broken ship and a way to preserve frog eggs. He scans the dunes of a seemingly empty Tatooine, searching for a way to defeat a dragon. He waits in the ancient ruins of Tython for the mysteries of the Force to be revealed, and finds himself responding instead to an Imperial attack. He walks amid the wreckage of his adopted home world, reverencing the storied lives of those who had come before.

Dialogue with mystery brings us back to taking that long, loving look at the real. Contemplation before action. It's as simple as stopping, looking, waiting. It's a disposition of patience and awe, allowing the natural world to unfold around us in answer to our spiritual searching, and making ourselves available to respond to whatever occurs. It's a willingness to be surprised and delighted by what we find in the thornbushes. We simply allow Mystery to speak to us. And then we listen.

We stay attentive to that quiet whisper of God.

But are we patient enough? Do we pause and linger in our daily pilgrimages? Or do we do nothing but rush ahead, missing our chances to learn and grow and experience joy?

PILGRIMAGE TO THE GALAXY'S EDGE

There was something poetic about standing in Star Wars: Galaxy's Edge, nestled deep within Disney's Hollywood Studios, with my dad.

It was another pilgrimage of sorts. The destination, of course, was significant. We were more than a little excited to be among the citizens of Batuu in a genuine immersion into the Star Wars galaxy. Everything looked so real, so authentic, and the whine of "TIE fighters" overhead made us glance to the skies.

But, like any pilgrimage, this wasn't just about *being there*. For me, it was a reminder of where I'd *been*. All those years ago. That old VHS machine. My dad's copy of the original trilogy. That fateful night when he said, "Let's watch this—I think you'll like it." And now, years later, we literally returned together to a new kind of Star Wars for the first time. My daughters—his granddaughters—were just as giddy as we were.

The old and the new. The tradition and the innovation. A look back so as to better see the road ahead.

In the shadow of the *Millennium Falcon*, my dad said, "Let's get in line. Smugglers Run only has a forty-minute wait." I glanced at my watch, well aware of our dinner reservations at Hollywood and Vine, all the way on the other side of the park.

"Sure," I said. And in we went.

The wait was much closer to ninety minutes, and we had to sprint to make those reservations. But the time in between, the time we waited and waited in line, taking tiny, shuffling steps throughout Ohnaka Transport Solutions, was time well spent. Sure, the details of that exhibit are amazing. We took pictures; we pointed things out; we looked stuff up.

Was the ride worth it? Yes, of course. It's a ton of fun.

But those ninety minutes with my dad weren't just about getting to the end of the line. They were an invitation to go backward in time, to settle into the nostalgia and the fantasies of a younger version of myself. They were an invitation, really, to look past the *Star Wars* of it all and sink into a father-son relationship that has deepened and evolved, to reflect back on what those old VHS tapes *pointed to* for me and my dad, not simply what they *were*. A movie, sure, but a shared experience, a shared love, an ongoing bond forged in a singular point in time but constantly renewed and revisited. ("Are you caught up on Ahsoka yet? No? Well, I won't spoil anything.")

Those ninety minutes were an opportunity to look ahead, too, to think how I might conjure up such a world for my daughters, and be grateful that my dad had done so for me. And all this *with* the man who had been there when it had all started, the one who lit that spark of love for Star Wars. What was next for our relationship in this ongoing pilgrimage?

It's easy to miss these kinds of moments. It's easy to hurry on to the end of the line. It's easy to think these things are unimportant. But if a ninety-minute wait in a line at Disney World for a Star Wars ride can hold spiritual significance, I bet there are a few pilgrim places right here, right now, *wherever* you are, that might surprise and delight you.

In the end, the disposition of a pilgrim is one who embraces the journey, who knows that the more we see, the more we're challenged, and the more we're able to imagine, the more we can hope for something new. And in the hope, we find the courage to believe that we might be part of it, that we have something worth saying, worth doing, something unique that only we can contribute.

Do we answer the call when a little astromech droid rolls into our lives and projects an image of someone summoning us to action? Do we embrace that pilgrimage?

For someone, somewhere, in need of *your* help, you just might be the only hope. How will you respond?

FULLY OPERATIONAL PILGRIMS

1. **Reach out.** Try to imagine your future: the next few moments, weeks, years. What feelings well up in you as you contemplate all that is to come?

2. **Set your intention.** A pilgrimage is a paradoxical thing: a solitary journey undertaken in community. Such an undertaking requires dialogue, with self and with others.

   Make your mantra by completing the following sentences: *As a pilgrim, I seek . . .* what? *As a pilgrim, I share . . .* what? Repeat that mantra several times. Be mindful of your breath.

3. **Review the past.** As you repeat your mantra, allow your mind to wander. Where does it go? Are you thinking of a moment from earlier today, earlier this year, or many years ago? How have you engaged fully in your life's pilgrimage? Where have you shrunk back from full engagement? What patterns from the past help you best prepare for the moments yet to come?

   Settle on a moment you hope for—one that has not yet come to pass. What insight does this moment reveal to you?

4. **Always in motion.** The moment you've settled on from your hoped-for future necessarily builds upon your past and present. What do you need to do to make this future moment a reality?

5. **This is the way.** How can a disposition toward hope inform your pilgrimage? Practice that hope now.

End your reflection by cultivating a disposition of gratitude to yourself, the universe, and the infinite Other.

PART 3 REPRISE

WHAT CHANCE, OR WHAT CHOICE?

The first phase of the Star Wars High Republic stories is set some two hundred years before *The Phantom Menace*. The galaxy is being terrorized by the Nihil, a gang of intergalactic space marauders. They're a collection of vicious beings, individuals who have been cast out of their homes, forced to make terrible choices, or simply dealt a tough hand in life.

From a certain point of view, the Nihil give them purpose. Individual members seek ways to advance within their ranks while simultaneously elevating the galactic profile and prowess of the Nihil as a whole and their leader, the Eye of the Nihil, Marchion Ro, in particular.

But Marchion Ro has his own goals and secrets, and ultimately every individual Nihil is expendable—as is every life he encounters. Planets are obliterated. Ships are pulled from hyperspace and destroyed. Foot soldiers are sent on suicidal missions; others are tricked into sacrificing themselves. The Nihil at the top of the pyramid, the Tempest Runners, stay alive only by constantly looking over their shoulders, prepared to both block a knife in the back and thrust one into the chest of a challenger.

This is no community. This is raw power exercised in and over living beings for personal gain—the Standard of the Enemy taken to its logical conclusion. Nothing else seems to matter.

It's hard to read the word *Nihil* and not immediately think of *nihilism*—a belief that life is void of any meaning or purpose. In such a world, and certainly in the world the Nihil inhabit, hope seems a far-off fantasy. How do you respond to such an outlook on life?

Jesuit priest and founder of Homeboy Industries Greg Boyle has spent much of his life working with gang members and former gang members in Los Angeles, California. "Gang violence itself is a language," he says. "It's not about the flying of bullets. It's about a lethal absence of hope. So let's address the despair."[84]

If this sort of violence, this way of being, is a *language*, how do we respond in a way that is meaningful and on point?

That's been the work of the third section of this book: exploring different spiritual tools and paths that might help us to breathe new hope into a world too often hampered by despair. For the Nihil, nothing really matters but power. When they fail, when they're killed off or left behind, they're forgotten.

The Jedi of the High Republic era are imperfect, to be sure, but they have a mantra: *For light and life.* They have a purpose and attach greater meaning to what they do and to the sacrifices they make. We might even say they follow a standard that they hold high, even when it's difficult and darkness presses in.

Light and life? Or power and darkness? Either way, there is a choice to be made.

When the Rebel leaders are prepared to give up in the face of the Death Star's power, Jyn Erso reminds all of us what sort of galaxy we might yet live in: it's not a matter of chance; it's a matter of choice.

"What chance do we have?" she repeats incredulously, echoing the doubts of those gathered around her. "The question is 'What choice?'" She fears that surrendering to such a powerful evil will result in a galaxy forever condemned and a life lived in fear and terror.

Hope can prove elusive. And it's tempting to think that nothing we do matters, that we have no ability to change the course of history. But history itself proves that thinking wrong. People who make clear, concrete choices for the good help advance society for everyone. They help lift others up. They help build a world that is more just, more peaceful.

It's not chance. It's choice. We might be tempted to think of fulfilling our destinies as something we inevitably trip into, but that's not the case at all. Whatever—*whomever*—we're made to be is the result of a lot of individual choices, and not always the right ones at all the right times. We can *choose* to hope. We can *choose* to do those things that create a future worth hoping in and living for. We can practice indifference and build up good institutions grounded in the best of our traditions. We can nourish our own inner pilgrim and treat others with curiosity and compassion, always mindful of our own inherent goodness. We're on this road of redemption together, calling out the best in one another and in the world itself, a road marked clearly by a standard that declares hope in light and life.

The enemy might be evil, might be powerful, might be overwhelming. But simple acts of hope prove the enemy has not yet won. And we are still standing. Still walking forward.

CONCLUSION: RHYME

"It's like poetry," George Lucas famously said. "They rhyme. Every stanza kind of rhymes with the last one."[85]

Reflecting on the prequel trilogy, Lucas was describing how his Star Wars stories fit together. There are parallels and callbacks and characters who step into similar roles. A young Anakin Skywalker, for example, is instrumental in blowing up the Trade Federation Droid Control Ship in the skies above Naboo in *The Phantom Menace*. That space station was no Death Star—it was no moon, either—but no one in the theater saw that scene and *didn't* think of Luke Skywalker's similar heroics in *A New Hope*. Starkiller Base, too, held a parallel place in the plot of *The Force Awakens*, and was destroyed in a similar way by another hotshot pilot. The callback to *A New Hope* was unmistakable.

It rhymes, I suppose. Like a stanza that makes you pause and look back at the one before; that forces you to remember it for the line ahead. What came before informs what comes after—new and different stories, and yet there are inescapable parallels and similarities. Patterns. We circle back before we move beyond. We build.

Is this not *exactly* how the ebbs and flows of the spiritual life work? Is this not what we've begun to glimpse in the Wayseeker Exercises throughout this book? Our life is necessarily informed by what has been; our present "rhymes" with our past and foreshadows our future. But if we do not develop the eyes to see this spiritual life unfolding there within us, these events appear random.

Rather than rhymes, they're just a lot of noise.

THE SLOW WORK

When *The Force Awakens* was released, a friend and I sat over a cup of coffee and debriefed.

"Why," I began, "did Starkiller Base need to be so similar to the Death Star? It was practically the same thing, just bigger!"

My friend smiled. "Think of your iPhone. How is it different now from five years ago? The technology hasn't completely changed; it's evolved. Progressed. They built upon what was. It only makes sense that it would bear resemblance to what's come before."[86]

I remember nodding. That made a lot of sense to me, and perhaps was obvious to other viewers of the film. Of course there wouldn't be this sudden break with the past; the story goes on, continuing to unfold, building upon what has been, beat after beat.

It not only rhymes but reflects a logical and necessary progression.

The lesson here for our spiritual lives is this: The pitfalls we encounter in our daily routines, those temptations and failures and bad habits, don't go away. We might defeat them for a time, but they come back stronger, different, and evolved. This is not a failure on our part but simply the natural flow of the spiritual life.

There was a lot of tragic wisdom in the words of Baylan Skoll. In the sixth episode of *Ahsoka*, the former Jedi, turning to his apprentice, Shin Hati, reflects on the galaxy's—or, galaxies'—tragic history. "It's all inevitable," he says. "The fall of the Jedi, rise of the Empire. It repeats again and again." Shin assumes it's now their turn to wield power, these dark Jedi. That power is in fact the only thing worth seeking. But Lord Baylan disagrees, noting how ephemeral such power really is. "What I seek is the beginning," he says, "so I may finally bring this cycle to an end."

We know Baylan cannot succeed, not completely at least: *Ahsoka* is sandwiched squarely in between *The Return of the Jedi* and *The Force Awakens*. The First Order takes the Empire's place. But this desire to return to the beginning, to simply start over—it's tempting. Would that we could erase all the missteps and failures, all the disorder and chaos, all the injustice and pettiness. Would that we could rid ourselves of the bad habits that plague us. And yet, we know that's impossible. It is our job to learn, to build, and to mend. And to recognize that, even after we've descended into the depths of ourselves, even when we emerge with new insight and vigor—our own manifestation of Ahsoka the White—we are greeted by the same temptations. We still have to be about the business of discernment, of muddling through life's daily choices and challenges.

How did the First Order rise from the ashes of the Empire? It was not because the heroes of the Rebellion failed to be *heroic enough*. They defeated the Empire. Sure, the Imperial Remnant held on in the Outer Rim and the

Unknown Regions. Thrawn did what Thrawn does, and space whales got involved. There were plots within plots. But it wasn't simply a failure to route evil. The natural resurgence of the same temptation that allowed evil to flourish in the first place—the constant pull of power, pride, and unhealthy possession—never truly goes away.

The ways in which we find ourselves uniquely susceptible to these things will likely prove consistent throughout our lives. The patterns of the spiritual life—those dueling spirits of fate—then become all the more important to discern. Because, when we fail or fall short, and when we feel as though all the lessons we've learned and hard work we've done have amounted to nothing, it is in this rhyming moment when we must recognize the whispers of the evil spirit. We are not perfect; our spiritual life is not a straight line but a labyrinthine path. All we need to do is commit to the forward path. Keep walking. Keep going. Keep working through the redemption we seek. Keep reaching out to take someone else by the hand and bring them along.

This is how the dark side is defeated: by simply continuing our slow, stumbling, steady trek toward the light.

GIVING TEMPTATION A NAME

The return of Emperor Palpatine in *The Rise of Skywalker* was something of a surprise. There wasn't a whole lot of groundwork laid for that plot point based on the two preceding movies. But taking the long view, which includes Palpatine's obsession with immortality and cloning, the ever-present threat of the Sith, and the carefully laid plans that have come to the fore in other Star Wars stories since, Palpatine's perverse resurrection makes sense.

This, too, rhymes. And it gives us another insight into the patterns of the spiritual life. We don't just grapple with temptation and would-be evil in the abstract; we grapple with *specific* temptations. Ignatius of Loyola reminds us to *name* them. To not allow the enemy of our human nature to pull us into a world of fog and secrecy. Because naming the threat and being specific robs it of power.

So Palpatine was the specific Sith that wound up beguiling everyone in the Skywalker saga. He came close to winning. But as soon as he revealed himself, as soon as Rey and Leia and all the others knew that they were dealing with this specter of the past, the series of events leading to Palpatine's final destruction were set in motion.

We all have a Palpatine character in our spiritual lives. Maybe more than one. That's okay. Name it—and then begin the work of overthrowing it. You won't win every round; none of us do. But remember that getting struck down isn't the end. It might just make you more powerful than you had previously imagined. You might begin to see who you really are, not to mention who you might yet become.

And remember that Rey had all the Jedi there, past and present, to help her see her own quest through. We, too, have a communion of saints—all the folks who have walked this path before us—to look to for inspiration, intercession, and aid. Who are the Force ghosts accompanying you on your journey?

HOPE AND BALANCE

What does it mean to bring balance to the Force? Did Anakin succeed in striking this galactic balance by capitulating to the dark side and becoming the terror known as Darth Vader? If so—and I think there's something to be said for that argument—it suggests that these patterns of light and dark in our spiritual lives are not problematic but in fact are necessary to strike balance in our own inner lives. We touch the darkness so as to know the light; we perceive the light as all the more bright for having experienced shadow. It's part of the journey.

A group of young Jesuit writers put together a delightfully insightful meme way back in 2012 that illustrates this ebb and flow between light and shadow. On one side of the graphic, we see Yoda; on the other, we see St. Paul. The text reads: "Fear leads to anger. Anger leads to hate. Hate leads to suffering. And 'affliction produces endurance, and endurance, proven character, and proven character, hope, and hope does not disappoint.'"[87] That final, non–Star Wars bit is from the New Testament: Romans 5:3–5.

Even when we find ourselves clouded by fear, hope is the inevitable endpoint *if* we are able to muddle on in spite of everything. "This is what hope *is*," says High Republic Jedi Master Stellan Gios in *The Fallen Star*. "It isn't pretending that nothing will go wrong if only we try hard enough. It's looking squarely at all the obstacles in the way—knowing the limits of our own power, and the possibility of failure—and moving ahead anyway. That is how we must proceed. With hope."[88]

SANDY FOUNDATIONS

We return to Tatooine, that dry, sandy planet that appears so often in Star Wars. It's where our journey in this book began. As we have seen, the settings and drama of Star Wars provide apt analogies to how we fail to live up to our own expectations—or those of others. Again and again, we may taste something of the dryness of that place in our spiritual life.

Remember back to the beginning of this spiritual journey: the sands of Tatooine are both temptation to paralysis and invitation to step beyond. Those tiny grains brush against your skin, beckoning you to look up and out and onward. To listen to the voices of desires welling up within you.

In this place, you begin your spiritual journey. But you return to it, too, many times over. This rhyming pattern is a reminder that the Spirit continues to create within you and within the world. You—the unique holy creature that you are—continue to have an essential role to play. Where are your deepest desires pointing you?

It is upon the foundation of those desires—a foundation built on hope—that we build something new, and from which we set out into the galaxy.

AFTERWORD: A STAR WAR

A final thought. After all this talk of spirituality and peace and compassion and hope, we might wonder with a growing sense of unease about the *war* part of these Star Wars. The seemingly necessary violence that undergirds the whole story. The glossing over of the fact that the pretend lightsabers we swung about as kids represented weapons that sliced through flesh just as easily as they skewered the metal arms of battle droids. The fact that those *pew-pew* sounds are blaster bolts that blow up buildings and lives, and that in each TIE fighter that goes spiraling into oblivion, a living being is *lost*. That for every noble Kenobi-esque sacrifice there are three dozen life stories snuffed out with barely a blink of the eye. That this violence is central to what our shared experience of a galaxy far, far away entails.

After our journey through spiritual possibilities of the Star Wars universe, can we dismiss this wanton destruction?

We believe that all things are redeemable, and that the Spirit of the universe pulses in every creature. The answer, then

(I hope), is no. Even when we face the evil of the dark side, violence and power and greed cannot be our knee-jerk response.

And yet, does another way exist? Can we stand up to evil without compromising our moral standards?

Knowing that only Sith deal in absolutes, we proceed with caution, with curiosity, and with a willingness to weigh all perspectives and insights. A definitive answer will probably remain beyond our grasp, but let us reach for one anyway. And let us hope that a third way will make itself known in the reaching.

A LOSE-LOSE PROPOSITION

"No longer certain that one ever does win a war, I am," Yoda admits in the sixth season of *The Clone Wars*. "For in fighting the battles, the bloodshed, already lost we have."

Yoda is not wrong. By leading the war efforts, the Jedi have caused suffering and death even while retaining the moniker of keepers of the peace. In the High Republic era, the Jedi refused to fire before being fired upon, which was super frustrating to a reader who just needed the Jedi to win. But how different that approach is from the Jedi leading battalions of clones into battle some two hundred years later!

In the final arc of *The Clone Wars* animated series, Rex, the beloved clone captain of the 501st, admits to Ahsoka Tano that he and his fellow clones have mixed feelings about the war. "Many people wished it never happened. But without it, we clones wouldn't exist."

How much more entangled in the systems of violence can one get? One's very existence is born out of, and is defined by, violence! And yet even here we glimpse the nuanced potential for good—dare we say, redemption?—tucked inside seemingly endless evil and suffering. Rex, who is a good man, stands up and steps forward. He does his duty. He protects the vulnerable and fights for the justice he hopes will prevail. And the lives he touches, the fellow clones whose hearts he changes, are just as real as his valor, sacrifice, and friendship. But, like all clones, Rex wrestles with whether his purpose goes *beyond* violence and conflict. Is there—can there be—a place for him in a galaxy at peace?

Unfortunately, he never gets to find out. Order 66 commences as soon as Rex finishes sharing his reflections on war with Ahsoka. And although Ahsoka helps Rex break free from his programming, the rise of the Empire from the ashes of the Republic immediately calls into question the very existence of clones. Rex finds himself fighting a new foe.

When you've known nothing but war, do you *keep* fighting even though the context and the players and the declaration of purpose have changed? That question takes center stage in *The Bad Batch*, the animated sequel series to *The Clone Wars*. Do they continue to wage war regardless of who is directing the battles? What do their lives even look like if they're not fighting? Are their lives their own to live? Or do they forever owe something to their warmongering benefactors? And if they choose to fight, what then? Do they support the Republic-turned-Empire, even though that Empire now stands for what they once fought against? Or do they stand against this new power, assuming the role of separatists or rebels—the very threat they sought to eradicate mere days or weeks or years earlier?

Good soldiers follow orders, we hear again and again in *The Bad Batch*. At first, it is given as a command, but slowly it takes on a new identity. It becomes a justification. A rationale for avoiding the tough questions about wars that are waged forever. It seduces good people, like the clones for whom we rooted for an entire animated series, to maintain an unquestioning position on a disconcerting status quo.

In the third episode of season 2 of *The Bad Batch*, a disillusioned Commander Cody asks the Bad Batch-turned-Imperial clone, Crosshair, "Are we making the galaxy better?" Cody's subsequent desertion from Imperial command makes clear the answer he has discerned. "We make our own choices," Cody insists. "And we have to live with them, too."

When we're caught up in the machine of war, it becomes nearly impossible to disentangle the threads of existence. The questions we pose take conflict as a given rather than probe whether death and destruction should even be on the table. We see no other way. Can there be a nonviolent path?

AN ENDLESS ESCALATION

In the first part of this book, we reflected on our own inner wounds. By now you've no doubt realized that we owe it to ourselves to consider how many of these wounds are the result of violence. But not all violence needs to be physical. How many of these wounds are inflicted due to some sort of verbal, emotional, or spiritual attack? Insults, self-deprecation, a culture of decreasing self-worth, online bullying. These, too, are forms of violence and can be just as destructive. Think back to chapter 4 on systems and structures; think of the violence done to communities—no weapon need be drawn!

"We were all raised in violence," writes peace activist and former Jesuit John Dear in his book *The Nonviolent Life*. "We are taught that violence is normal, the way of the world, the way of life. We have no inkling that life could be otherwise. It is only natural that we internalize that violence done to us as children. If we do not explore and call out that legacy of violence, we will continue to do violence to ourselves and others."[89]

Clearly, we don't need to enlist in some intergalactic war to get caught up in the violence done to our world! Looking at others with an eye of judgment, using language that evokes harm, and thinking ill of ourselves are all forms of violence to which we've become desensitized. From the seeds of this numbness grow spiritual weeds.

In another book, *Living Peace: A Spirituality of Contemplation and Action*, Dear writes, "The culture of violence would have us believe that just as we are violent, God must also be violent. . . . Instead of God the peacemaker, we have been taught to believe in god the warmaker. . . . Because of this, many reject God. Who would want anything to do with such a terrifying prospect of 'divine violence?'"[90]

Who indeed!

There are no easy answers to violence and suffering. Good people serve courageously in armed forces around the world and protect the safety of communities large and small. At the same time, there are many people and entire communities who do not feel safe. There are people who don't feel that they can turn to authorities for protection and consequently take up arms, adopting violent means for mere survival. And there are those struggling under oppressive regimes who see no way out except through the path of violence, death, and destruction. This is simply the world we live in, and I do not presume to have answers to these snowballing tragedies.

Yes, context matters. But wouldn't it be nice to at least be able to *imagine* a world where structural violence—guns and tanks and nuclear warheads baked into the construction and maintenance of societal order—isn't necessary? And how far we are from such imaginative potential when we reduce our spirituality and whatever word we use for *God* to be no more than a blesser of wars!

"If we do not address the violence in the world, our inner peace is an empty illusion," Dear continues. "Likewise, we cannot seek peace publicly and expect to help disarm the world while our hearts are filled with violence, judgment, and rage."[91]

BURNING AWAY

In perhaps one of the greatest monologues of the entire Star Wars franchise, the spymaster of *Andor*, Luthen Rael, lays out plainly the cost of the Rebellion. Luthen sacrifices his very soul to prop up the fledgling rebel cause. He employs the tools of his enemy. "I burn my life to make a sunrise that I know I'll never see," he laments.

He, too, is a victim of a violent system. He, too, is unable to extract himself, or envision a way forward that does not necessitate violence.

And perhaps he is right. Perhaps there isn't a way to overthrow the Empire without the shedding of blood. Clearly, Luthen has come to that conclusion, but he's not happy about it. He knows he's forfeited some fundamental part of what it means to be human, to be alive.

What does that kind of self-sacrifice do to a person? How does someone of this commitment emerge on the other side, in a peaceful society that has transcended the Empire?

I don't know the answer. But I know it is not easy. This arms race of violent extremism has no logical end but in the complete and utter annihilation of the enemy. (And someone is always making a buck off the sale of more and more arms—remember the crowd on Canto Bight and Finn's reluctant discovery that both the First Order *and* the Resistance sought these folks to fund the war effort?) Think of how broken the Empire was when they were finally defeated at Jakku, a whole year after the destruction of the second Death Star—and even then, they fought on, wasting lives and resources! Rather than seek peace, they fought until there was nothing and no one left. That's how twisted our rationale becomes in this system of violence.

Either we win it all and we win it our way, or we burn ourselves and everything in reach to the ground. It's worth reflecting on the Emperor's contingency plan in the case of his death. Step one was Operation: Cinder, a galaxy-wide campaign of genocidal destruction on Imperial and non-Imperial worlds alike. The goal? Sow chaos and death and ensure no one claimed his mantle of power. Again, Sith deal in absolutes. It's the dark side that can find no compromise, no accommodation, no common ground upon which to build from shared humanity and experience. That's the enemy's Standard.

In a sarcastic, biting retort from the great series of books *Star Wars: The New Jedi Order*—now relegated to "Legends" status and no longer considered canon—Han Solo imagines how the Empire would have responded to the invasion of the mysterious, powerful, and deadly alien species known as the Yuuzhan Vong.

> "What the Empire would have done was build a supercolossal Yuuzhan Vong–killing battle machine. They would have called it the Nova Colossus or the Galaxy Destructor or the Nostril of Palpatine or something equally grandiose. They would have spent billions of credits, employed thousands of contractors and subcontractors, and equipped it with the latest in death-dealing technology. And you know what would have happened? *It wouldn't have worked.* They'd forget to bolt down a metal plate over an access hatch leading to the main reactors, or some other mistake, and a hotshot enemy pilot would drop a bomb down there and *blow the whole thing up.*"[92]

More and more violence. A refusal to seek out a third way. The very epitome of a Standard that reflects wealth, privilege, and power. The ongoing march to more security, safety, and prosperity that necessitates a never-ending accumulation of power and weaponry to outgun a would-be opponent. That's the solution of empire. That's the solution of *the* Empire. And that's the solution we too readily reach for, even though we know it can't possibly keep us safe and it can't possibly end the violence and uncertainty and danger.

And yet, we give in to our fear even though we know where fear leads, which is to the same place as dealing in absolutes.

THE NOT-BATTLE OF CRAIT

In all the promotional materials for *The Last Jedi*, we were told things weren't going to go the way we expected. As it turned out, this proved to be true.

In what is perhaps one of the most surprising scenes, Luke Skywalker projects himself through the Force from Ahch-To all the way to Crait. There he confronts his nephew, Kylo Ren, in what I expected would be an epic showdown. Weren't we *all* expecting a lightsaber duel and the chance to see the great Jedi Master once more wield his legendary laser sword?

But blades never crossed. And, as we learned, the threat of violence between the two was never actually real. Kylo couldn't have hit Luke even if he'd been able to land a blow, and Luke was unable to destroy his nephew because he wasn't really *there* at all.

This was an example of nonviolence masquerading as its opposite. A subverting of expectations. What appeared to be violence was its opposite. Nonviolence appearing in unexpected places necessitates a different kind of courage and skillset but the same kind of sacrifice. Nonviolence allows others to escape with their lives, giving them the chance to make new choices. John Dear explains:

> "Nonviolence confronts systemic injustice with active love but refuses to retaliate with further violence under any circumstances. In order to halt the vicious cycle of violence, it requires a willing acceptance of suffering and death rather than inflicting suffering or death on anyone else. The art of nonviolence lies in the mastery of dying, not killing."[93]

This sounds an awful lot like what we saw Luke do. In standing up to injustice with love rather than anger, and in bringing a willingness to accept his own death to give both his nephew and the Resistance the opportunity to keep going, Luke exhibited a mastery in personal sacrifice and a devotion to the greater good.

Love manifesting itself in self-sacrificing deeds.

This is where hope leads us. We insist that there must be another way, a third way, some nonviolent path that disrupts the status quo. There must be a path that resolutely stands up to injustice and evil and destruction while not giving in and becoming what we seek to destroy.

"It was said that you would destroy the Sith, not join them!" Obi-Wan screams at his fallen Padawan in the final moments of *Revenge of the Sith*. We hear the echo of his words as we make choices for peace and justice, light and life, or power, privilege, violence, and darkness.

Let us not become what we seek to destroy. We must remain ever-mindful of the spiritual world that pulses all around us.

I hope there's been an awakening—in you, in me, in the very fabric of our world itself. Let us respond to what has stirred within us. Let us see where this new Spirit might lead. Let us imagine a better world, one built on hope.

ACKNOWLEDGMENTS

This book began as a feisty email exchange. My friend and editor, Gary Jansen, had taken the unenviable position that the Disney+ series, *Obi-Wan Kenobi*, was not very good. I disagreed. Back and forth we went until I casually pitched the idea of a Star Wars and Ignatian spirituality book. He went to the mat for that idea—and the proposal that followed. And here we are. Thanks, Gary, for your passion and your faith that I could pull this off.

The seeds of this book were planted in other times and other places, too. My dad, Matthew Clayton, was the one who first showed me the films. Those old VHS tapes are still in his closet to this day. He took me to see the Special Edition versions in theaters and insists he's caught up on all the live-action TV shows. My mom, Joanne Clayton, has kindly provided a home to a not insignificant amount of Star Wars toys, books, video games, and LEGO sets over the years. Same house, different closet from those VHS tapes. I've not yet been charged rent and *promise* that one day I'll move them.

My brother, Alex Clayton, has added to my still growing collection of Star Wars LEGO, Pop Funkos, and more. It's nice that *someone* understands.

Earlier versions of some of these chapters appeared or have been workshopped elsewhere. Parts of "Chapter 4: Structures" were first written for IgnatianSpirituality.org and their annual Lenten campaign to promote the Spiritual Exercises. Thanks to Denise Gorss for seeing the potential.

Parts of "Chapter 5: Caves" came from an article I wrote for *National Catholic Reporter* in celebration of the aforementioned excellent TV show, *Obi-Wan Kenobi*. The article is titled "The Redemption of Obi-Wan Kenobi." I am always grateful to the folks at NCR, especially Stephanie Yeagle and Shannon Evans, who allow me to reflect out loud about pop culture and spirituality.

The initial draft for "Chapter 7: Edits" was a project I worked on in a spiritual nonfiction class, taught by Jon Malesic. His feedback was invaluable. A version of "Chapter 8: Two" was my final project for a course on the Spiritual Exercises taught at Creighton University by my friend, Dr. Eileen Burke-Sullivan. She encouraged me to not let the essay die on my desktop.

I am grateful to my colleagues and friends at the Jesuit Conference of Canada and the United States for encouraging me in my writing and thinking, and giving me space and a platform with which to write and think and pray. I am grateful, too, to my fellow pilgrims from Creighton University and Regis University who visited the Ignatian places in Spain and Rome. It was on that trip that I met Fr. Kevin Burke, SJ, who is quoted in this book, and Tom Murray, who was the first to suggest to me that my writing on Star Wars and Ignatian spirituality might actually be useful to someone.

My friend Patrick Sullivan—also quoted in these pages—has my deepest appreciation for his careful, thorough, and thoughtful read-through of the very first draft. His deep knowledge of Star Wars lore, Ignatian spirituality, and theology was invaluable. Thanks, too, to my friend Jonathan Tomick, who was an advocate and supporter of this project from proposal to final draft, and whose insights into the craft of writing I always value.

Thanks, too, to my editor at Loyola Press, Maura Poston, who immersed herself in the Star Wars galaxy just to provide the wonderfully helpful line edits that ultimately shaped the manuscript into the book you now hold.

I want to thank two spiritual mentors from my time at Fairfield University who over the years have become good friends and sources of support in the Ignatian tradition. Carolyn Rusiackas has been a tireless advocate for my writing, always ready with words of support and a listening ear. Fr. Jim Bowler, SJ, my spiritual director, has walked with me through the spiritual tradition that gave this book life, helping me make sense of God in my own days so that I can hopefully help others find God in theirs.

For my own two Padawans, Elianna and Camira: it is a joy and a delight to pass on to you a story that has meant so much to me. Please be careful with my LEGO sets. They're toys—but not really.

And to Alli, who—by her own admission—is no big Star Wars fan. You played a pivotal role in the crafting of this book. There were many nights of cooking dinner and workshopping concepts, and even when you didn't know the characters, the planets, or the idiosyncrasies of the Force, you could pinpoint the themes that mattered—and made them better, more accessible, more relevant. Thank you for your wisdom, for your encouragement, for your love, for watching all of *Andor* with me, for both purchasing and permitting the hanging of numerous pieces of Star Wars art, and for reigniting my slight obsession with Star Wars LEGO.

ENDNOTES

1. Joseph Campbell, *The Hero with a Thousand Faces*, 3rd ed. (Novato, CA: New World Library, 2008), 7.

2. Chris Taylor, *How Star Wars Conquered the Universe: The Past, Present, and Future of a Multibillion Dollar Franchise* (New York: Basic Books, 2014), 58.

3. Ignatius was also one of the founders of the Society of Jesus, better known as the Jesuits, a worldwide religious order of Catholic priests and brothers.

4. Cass R. Sunstein, *The World according to Star Wars* (New York: HarperCollins, 2016), 65.

5. Richard Rohr, *The Universal Christ: How a Forgotten Reality Can Change Everything We See, Hope for, and Believe* (New York: Convergent Books/Penguin Random House, 2019), 51.

6. Matthew Bortolin, *The Dharma of Star Wars* (Somerville, MA: Wisdom Publications, 2005, 2015), 3.

7. Bortolin, *The Dharma*, 3.

8. Bortolin, *The Dharma*, 9.

9. "Prayer of Teilhard de Chardin," https://www.ignatianspirituality.com/prayer-of-teilhard-de-chardin/.

10. Dean Brackley, *The Call to Discernment in Troubled Times: New Perspectives on the Transformative Wisdom of Ignatius of Loyola* (New York: Crossroad Publishing Company, 2004), 247.

11. Brackley, *The Call to Discernment*, 246.

12. Walter Burghardt, "Contemplation: A Long Loving Look at the Real," in *An Ignatian Spirituality Reader*, ed. George W. Traub, SJ (Chicago: Loyola Press, 2008), 93.

13. Joseph Whelan, SJ, "Fall in Love," IgnatianSpirituality.com, https://www.ignatianspirituality.com/ignatian-prayer/prayers-by-st-ignatius-and-others/fall-in-love/.

14. "The Last Battle." IMDB. https://www.imdb.com/title/tt6050876/?ref_=tt_ch. See also "Meet Kanan, the Cowboy Jedi," YouTube Video, 2:28, https://www.youtube.com/watch?v=oXuFi2vH_PQ.

15. John Jackson Miller, *Star Wars: A New Dawn* (New York: Del Rey/Random House, 2015).

16. "Meet Kanan." https://www.youtube.com/watch?v=oXu Fi2vH_PQ. See also "Dave Filoni," Lucasfilm Ltd., https://www.lucasfilm.com/leadership/dave-filoni/.

17. Dan Brooks, "Fates Fulfilled: Dave Filoni Reflects on *Star Wars Rebels* Season Two, Part 2," StarWars.com, published September 13, 2016, https://www.starwars.com/news/fates-fulfilled-dave-filoni-reflects-on-star-wars-rebels-season-two-part-2.

18. Check out my book *Cannonball Moments: Telling Your Story, Deepening Your Faith* (Chicago: Loyola Press, 2022) for an in-depth exploration.

19. Richard C. Schwartz, PhD, *No Bad Parts: Healing Trauma and Restoring Wholeness with the Internal Family Systems Model* (Boulder, CO: Sounds True, 2021), 9.

20. Henri Nouwen, *The Wounded Healer*, quoted in Robert Durback ed., *Seeds of Hope: A Henri Nouwen Reader* (New York: Bantam Books, 1989), 55.

21. Parts of this chapter are taken from Eric Clayton, "Darth Vader and the First Week of the Spiritual Exercises," Ignatian Spirituality.com, published on March 16, 2022, https://www.ignatianspirituality.com/darth-vader-and-the-first-week-of-the-spiritual-exercises/.

22. Brackley, *The Call to Discernment*, 24.

23. While it's more helpful for us to think of these "weeks" as spiritual "movements" not confined to a standard length of time, it is worth noting that Jesuits typically make the Exercises over the course of one month during their formation. So, four weeks.

24. Brackley, *The Call to Discernment*, 93.

25. Brackley, *The Call to Discernment*, 98.

26. Brackley, *The Call to Discernment*, 104.

27. Brackley, *The Call to Discernment*, 105.

28. Richard Rohr, *Just This* (Albuquerque, NM: Center for Action and Contemplation, 2018), 88.

29. Rohr, *Just This*, 89.

30. Rohr, *Just This*, 95.

31. Judith Barad, "The Aspiring Jedi's Handbook of Virtue" in Kevin S. Decker and Jason T. Eberl, eds., *Star Wars and Philosophy: More Powerful Than You Can Possibly Imagine* (Chicago: Open Court Publishing, 2005), 63.

32. Ignatius of Loyola, *The Spiritual Exercises and Selected Works*, ed. George E. Ganss, SJ (New York: Paulist Press, 1991), no. 24.

33. Barad, "The Aspiring Jedi's Handbook of Virtue," 63.

34. Parts of this section are taken from my NCR essay "The Redemption of Obi-Wan Kenobi," June 25, 2022, https://www.ncronline.org/news/opinion/redemption-obi-wan-kenobi.

35. Ignatius of Loyola, *The Spiritual Exercises of St. Ignatius*, trans. and ed. Louis J. Puhl (Westminster, MD: The Newman Press, 1955), no. 326.

36. Ignatius of Loyola, *The Spiritual Exercises of St. Ignatius*, no. 335.

37. Jim McDermott, SJ, "The Gospel According to Star Wars," interview with AMDG, SoundCloud audio, 52:22. https://soundcloud.com/jesuitconference/the-gospel-according-to-star-wars-fr-jim-mcdermott-sj-on-faith-compassion-hope.

38. Matthew 5:48.

39. Ignatius of Loyola, *The Spiritual Exercises and Selected Works*, ed. George E. Ganss, SJ (New York: Paulist Press, 1991), no. 327.

40. Adam Christopher, *Star Wars: Shadow of the Sith* (New York: Random House Worlds, 2022), 450–51.

41. Drew Karpyshyn, *Star Wars: Darth Bane: Path of Destruction* (Del Rey/Ballantine Books, 2006), 289.

42. Ignatius of Loyola, *The Spiritual Exercises of St. Ignatius,* no. 146.

43. Ronald D. Siegel, *The Extraordinary Gift of Being Ordinary: Finding Happiness Right Where You Are* (New York: Guilford Press, 2022), 113.

44. Siegel, *The Extraordinary Gift,* 116.

45. Edward Gross and Mark A. Altman, *Secrets of the Force: The Complete, Uncensored, Unauthorized Oral History of Star Wars* (New York: St. Martin's Press, 2021), 205.

46. Jim Manney, *What Do You Really Want?: St. Ignatius Loyola and the Art of Discernment* (Huntington, IN: Our Sunday Visitor, 2015), 52.

47. Kevin O'Brien, SJ, *The Ignatian Adventure: Experiencing the Spiritual Exercises of St. Ignatius in Daily Life* (Chicago: Loyola Press, 2011), 67.

48. Manney, *What Do You Really Want?,* 53.

49. Matthew Bortolin, *The Zen of R2-D2: Ancient Wisdom from a Galaxy Far, Far Away* (Somerville, MA: Wisdom Publications, 2019), 13.

50. Bortolin, *The Zen of R2-D2,* 14.

51. Hieromonk Damascene, *Christ the Eternal Tao* (Platina, CA: St. Herman Press, 2004), 322.

52. Thomas Merton, *The Way of Chuang Tzu* (New York: New Directions, 2010), 28.

53. Damascene, *Christ the Eternal,* 323.

54. Bortolin, *The Zen of R2-D2,* 52.

55. Gregory Boyle, *The Whole Language: The Power of Extravagant Tenderness* (New York: Avid Reader/Simon and Schuster, 2021), 18.

56. Ignatius of Loyola, *The Spiritual Exercises of St. Ignatius,* no. 23.

57. Ibid.

58. Ibid, no. 234.

59. Delilah S. Dawson, *Inquisitor: Ride of the Red Blade* (New York: Random House Worlds, 2023), 7.

60. Claudia Gray, *Star Wars: The High Republic: Into the Dark* (Los Angeles: Lucasfilm Press, 2021), 33.

61. Claudia Gray, *The Fallen Star* (Glendale, CA: Lucasfilm Press, 2021), 139.

62. Gray, *The Fallen Star,* 139, 69.

63. Ignatius of Loyola, *The Spiritual Exercises of St. Ignatius*, no. 23, no. 155.

64. Bortolin, *The Zen of R2-D2,* 79.

65. Jennifer Vosters, "In an Age of Institutional Failure, 'Star Wars' Is Saving My Faith," *National Catholic Reporter*, December 5, 2020, https://www.ncronline.org/news/opinion/age-institutional-failure-star-wars-saving-my-faith.

66. Vosters, "In an Age."

67. Andrew Dyce, "Star Wars REALLY Wants You to Know the Sith Are Yoda's Fault," Screen Rant, May 9, 2019, https://screenrant.com/star-wars-sith-return-yodas-fault/.

68. Dyce, "Star Wars REALLY Wants You to Know."

69. *The Clone Wars*, season 6, episode 11, "Voices," directed by Danny Keller and Dave Filoni, written by George Lucas and Christian Taylor, aired March 7, 2014 in streaming service, Netflix.

70. Delilah S. Dawson, *Galaxy's Edge: Black Spire* (New York: Del Rey/Random House, 2019), 71.

71. Dawson, *Galaxy's Edge,* 71.

72. Francis. *Fratelli Tutti* [Encyclical Letter on Fraternity and Social Friendship], The Holy See, October 3, 2020, section 32.

73. Ignatius of Loyola, *The Spiritual Exercises of St. Ignatius*, no. 353.

74. Gray, *The Fallen Star,* 96.

75. Claudia Gray, *Star Wars: Bloodline* (New York: Del Rey/Random House, 2016), 249.

76. Gray, *Bloodline,* 203.

77. Eric Clayton, "'Star Wars: Andor' Shows Us Hope in the Darkness," *National Catholic Reporter*, December 3, 2022, https://www.ncronline.org/culture/star-wars-andor-shows-us-hope-darkness.

78. "No one has greater love than this, to lay down one's life for one's friends" (John 15:13).

79. O'Brien, *The Ignatian Adventure*, 248.

80. Ignatius of Loyola, *The Spiritual Exercises of St. Ignatius*, no. 230, no. 231.

81. Gustavo Gutiérrez, *A Theology of Liberation: History, Politics, and Salvation*, Rev. ed. (Maryknoll, NY: Orbis Books, 1988), 110.

82. Eric Sundrup, SJ, "Day Two: Arantzazu," *America Magazine,* October 17, 2018, https://www.americamagazine.org/journeys/2018/10/17/day-two-arantzazu.

83. Gross and Altman, *Secrets of the Force*, 544.

84. Greg Boyle, "Priest Responds to Gang Members' 'Lethal Absence of Hope' with Jobs, and Love," interview with Terry Gross, National Public Radio, *Fresh Air,* November 13, 2017, https://www.npr.org/2017/11/13/563734736/priest-responds-to-gang-members-lethal-absence-of-hope-with-jobs-and-love.

85. "It's Like Poetry, They Rhyme," YouTube Video, 0:23, December 30, 2015, https://www.youtube.com/watch?v=yFqFLo_bYq0.

86. Thanks to friend and fellow Star Wars nerd Patrick Sullivan!

87. "Week(s) in Review—August 12–September 2, 2022," *The Jesuit Post,* September 2, 2022. https://thejesuitpost.org/2012/09/weeks-in-review-august-12- september-2-2012/.

88. Gray, *The Fallen Star*, 190.

89. John Dear, *The Nonviolent Life* (Corvallis, OR: Pace e Bene Press, 2013), 27.

90. John Dear, *Living Peace: A Spirituality of Contemplation and Action* (New York: Image Books/Doubleday, 2001), 45.

91. Dear, *Living Peace*, 14–15.

92. Walter Jon Williams, *Destiny's Way (Star Wars: The New Jedi Order)*, reissue ed. (New York: Random House Worlds, 2003), 7.

93. Dear, *Living Peace*, 82.

BIBLIOGRAPHY

Barad, Judith. "The Aspiring Jedi's Handbook of Virtue." In *Star Wars and Philosophy: More Powerful Than You Can Possibly Imagine.* Edited by Kevin S. Decker and Jason T. Eberl. Chicago: Open Court Publishing, 2005.

Bortolin, Matthew. *The Dharma of Star Wars.* Somerville, MA: Wisdom Publications, 2005.

———. *The Zen of R2-D2: Ancient Wisdom from a Galaxy Far, Far Away.* Somerville, MA: Wisdom Publications, 2019.

Boyle, Gregory. "Priest Responds to Gang Members' 'Lethal Absence of Hope' with Jobs, and Love." Interview with Terry Gross. *Fresh Air.* National Public Radio. November 13, 2017. https://www.npr.org/2017/11/13/563734736/priest-responds-to-gang-members-lethal-absence-of-hope-with-jobs- and-love.

———. *The Whole Language: The Power of Extravagant Tenderness.* New York: Avid Reader/Simon and Schuster, 2021.

Brackley, Dean. *The Call to Discernment in Troubled Times: New Perspectives on the Transformative Wisdom of Ignatius of Loyola.* New York: Crossroad Publishing Company, 2004.

Brooks, Dan. "Fates Fulfilled: Dave Filoni Reflects on *Star Wars Rebels* Season Two, Part 2," StarWars.com. September 13, 2016. https://www.starwars.com/news/fates-fulfilled-dave-filoni-reflects-on-star-wars-rebels-season-two-part-2.

Burghardt, Walter. "Contemplation: A Long Loving Look at the Real." In *An Ignatian Spirituality Reader*. Edited by George W. Traub, SJ. Chicago: Loyola Press, 2008.

Campbell, Joseph. *The Hero with a Thousand Faces*. 3rd ed. Novato, CA: New World Library, 2008.

Christopher, Adam. *Star Wars: Shadow of the Sith*. New York: Random House Worlds, 2022.

Clayton, Eric A. *Cannonball Moments: Telling Your Story, Deepening Your Faith*. Chicago: Loyola Press, 2022.

———. "Darth Vader and the First Week of the Spiritual Exercises." IgnatianSpirituality.com. March 16, 2022. https://www.ignatianspirituality.com/darth-vader-and-the-first-week-of- the-spiritual-exercises/.

———. "The Redemption of Obi-Wan Kenobi." *National Catholic Reporter*. June 25, 2022. https://www.ncronline.org/news/opinion/redemption-obi-wan-kenobi.

———. "'Star Wars: Andor' Shows Us Hope in the Darkness." *National Catholic Reporter*. December 3, 2022. https://www.ncronline.org/culture/star-wars-andor-shows- us-hope-darkness.

The Clone Wars. Season 6, episode 11. "Voices." Directed by Danny Keller and Dave Filoni. Written by George Lucas and Christian Taylor. Featuring Tom Kane, Liam Neeson and Matt Lanter. Aired March 7, 2014, in streaming service. Netflix.

Damascene, Hieromonk. *Christ the Eternal Tao*. Platina, CA: St. Herman Press, 2004.

"Dave Filoni." Lucasfilm Ltd. https://www.lucasfilm.com/leadership/dave-filoni/.

Dawson, Delilah S. *Inquisitor: Ride of the Red Blade*. New York: Random House Worlds, 2023.

———. *Star Wars: Galaxy's Edge: Black Spire*. New York: Del Rey/Random House, 2019.

Dear, John. *Living Peace: A Spirituality of Contemplation and Action*. New York: Image Books/Doubleday, 2001.

———. *The Nonviolent Life*. Corvallis, OR: Pace e Bene Press, 2013.

Durback, Robert, ed. *Seeds of Hope: A Henri Nouwen Reader*. New York: Bantam Books, 1989.

Dyce, Andrew. "Star Wars REALLY Wants You to Know the Sith Are Yoda's Fault." *Screen Rant.* May 9, 2019. https://screenrant.com/star-wars-sith-return-yodas-fault/.

Francis. *Fratelli Tutti* [Encyclical Letter on Fraternity and Social Friendship]. The Holy See. October 3, 2020.

Gray, Claudia. *Star Wars: Bloodline.* New York: Del Rey/ Random House, 2016.

———. *Star Wars: The Fallen Star.* New York: Random House Worlds, 2022.

———. *Star Wars: Into the Dark.* Los Angeles: Lucasfilm Press, 2021.

Gross, Edward and Mark A. Altman. *Secrets of the Force: The Complete, Uncensored, Unauthorized Oral History of Star Wars.* New York: St. Martin's Press, 2021.

Gutiérrez, Gustavo. *A Theology of Liberation: History, Politics, and Salvation.* Rev. ed. Maryknoll, NY: Orbis Books, 1988.

Ignatius of Loyola. *The Spiritual Exercises and Selected Works.* Edited by George E. Ganss, SJ. New York: Paulist Press, 1991.

———. *The Spiritual Exercises of St. Ignatius.* Translated and edited by Louis J. Puhl. Westminster, MD: The Newman Press, 1955.

"It's Like Poetry, They Rhyme," YouTube Video, 0:23, December 30, 2015. https://www.youtube.com/watch?v=yFqFLo_bYq0.

Karpyshyn, Drew. *Star Wars: Darth Bane: Path of Destruction.* Del Rey/Ballantine Books, 2006.

"The Last Battle." IMDB. https://www.imdb.com/title/tt6050876/?ref_=tt_ch.

Manney, Jim. *What Do You Really Want?: St. Ignatius Loyola and the Art of Discernment.* Huntington, IN: Our Sunday Visitor, 2015.

McDermott, Jim. "The Gospel according to Star Wars." Interview with *AMDG.* SoundCloud audio, 52:22. https://soundcloud.com/jesuit-conference/the-gospel-according-to-star-wars-fr-jim-mcdermott-sj-on-faith-compassion-hope.

"Meet Kanan, the Cowboy Jedi." YouTube Video, 2:28. https://www.youtube.com/watch?v=oXuFi2vH_PQ.

Merton, Thomas. *The Way of Chuang Tzu.* New York: New Directions, 2010.

Miller, John Jackson. *Star Wars: A New Dawn*. New York: Del Rey/ Random House, 2015.

O'Brien, Kevin, SJ. *The Ignatian Adventure: Experiencing the Spiritual Exercises of St. Ignatius in Daily Life*. Chicago: Loyola Press, 2011.

"Prayer of Teilhard de Chardin." IgnatianSpirituality.com. https://www. ignatianspirituality.com/prayer-of-theilhard-de-chardin/

Rohr, Richard. *Just This: Prompts and Practices for Contemplation*. Albuquerque, NM: Center for Action and Contemplation, 2018.

———. *The Universal Christ: How a Forgotten Reality Can Change Everything We See, Hope for, and Believe*. New York: Convergent Books/Penguin Random House, 2019.

Schwartz, Richard C., PhD. *No Bad Parts: Healing Trauma and Restoring Wholeness with the Internal Family Systems Model*. Boulder, CO: Sounds True, 2021.

Scott, Cavan. *Dooku: Jedi Lost*. New York: Del Rey/Random House, 2021.

Siegel, Ronald D. *The Extraordinary Gift of Being Ordinary*. New York: Guilford Press, 2022.

Sundrup, Eric. "Day Two: Arantzazu." *America Magazine*. October 17, 2018. https://www.americamagazine.org/ journeys/2018/10/17/ day-two-arantzazu.

Sunstein, Cass R. *The World according to Star Wars*. New York: HarperCollins, 2016.

Taylor, Chris. *How Star Wars Conquered the Universe: The Past, Present, and Future of a Multibillion Dollar Franchise*. New York: Basic Books, 2014.

Vosters, Jennifer. In an Age of Institutional Failure, 'Star Wars' Is Saving My Faith." *National Catholic Reporter*. December 5, 2020. https://www.ncronline.org/news/opinion/age-institutional-failure-star-wars-saving-my-faith.

Tzu, Lao. *Tao Te Ching*. Translated by Gia-Fu Feng and Jane English. https://www.wussu.com/laotzu/laotzu07.html.

"Week(s) in Review—August 12–September 2, 2022." *The Jesuit Post*. September 2, 2022. https://thejesuitpost.org/2012/09/weeks-in-review-august-12-september-2-2012/.

Whelan, Joseph. "Fall in Love." IgnatianSpirituality.com. https://www. ignatianspirituality.com/ignatian-prayer/prayers-by-st-ignatius-and-others/fall-in-love/.

ABOUT THE AUTHOR

Eric A. Clayton grew up playing *Rogue Squadron* and *Shadows of the Empire* on Nintendo 64. Eric is exceedingly proud of his nearly complete (Yoda!) collection of the Micro Machine Star Wars heads that still reside in his childhood home. He spent a good portion of his childhood reading the *New Jedi Order* book series; nevertheless, he contends that James Luceno's *Darth Plagueis* is some of the best Star Wars literature out there—canon or not. To date, he has been emotionally unable to sit through the *Star Wars Holiday Special* in its entirety, though he proudly wears the Life Day t-shirt that was gifted to him from Galaxy's Edge. And May the 4th is a holiday his family observes without fail.

Eric is the award-winning author of *Cannonball Moments: Telling Your Story, Deepening Your Faith* (Loyola Press, 2022). Eric also serves as deputy director of communications at the Jesuit Conference of Canada and the United States. In this role, he writes "Now Discern This," a weekly column on Ignatian spirituality and storytelling, and co-hosts

"AMDG: A Jesuit Podcast." His essays on spirituality, parenting, and pop culture have appeared in *National Catholic Reporter*, *America Magazine*, *US Catholic*, *Busted Halo*, *Give Us This Day*, and *Dork Side of the Force*. His speculative fiction has been published by, among others, Black Hare Press, Medusa Tales Magazine, and Small Wonders Magazine. He is a sought-after speaker, facilitator, and retreat leader.

Eric has worked for and with several international faith-based organizations, including Catholic Relief Services, Maryknoll Lay Missioners, and the Sisters of Bon Secours. Eric was also an adjunct professor in the Mass Communication Department at Towson University. After graduating from Fairfield University, where he studied creative writing and international studies, Eric spent just under a year as a volunteer in Bolivia with the Salesians. He received his MA from American University in international media and earned a certificate in the Ignatian tradition from Creighton University.

Eric lives just outside of Baltimore, Maryland, with his wife, Alli, his two daughters, Elianna and Camira, and Sebastian, the family cat.

Subscribe to Eric's writing at ericclayton.substack.com and keep up with new projects at ericclaytonwrites.com.

PATIENT TRUST

Above all, trust in the slow work of God.
We are quite naturally impatient in everything to reach
    the end without delay.
We should like to skip the intermediate stages.
We are impatient of being on the way to something
    unknown, something new.

And yet it is the law of all progress
that it is made by passing through some stages of
    instability—
and that it may take a very long time.

And so I think it is with you;
your ideas mature gradually—let them grow,
let them shape themselves, without undue haste.
Don't try to force them on,
as though you could be today what time

(that is to say, grace and circumstances acting on your
    own good will)
will make of you tomorrow.

Only God could say what this new spirit
gradually forming within you will be.
Give Our Lord the benefit of believing
that his hand is leading you,
and accept the anxiety of feeling yourself
in suspense and incomplete.

—Pierre Teilhard de Chardin, SJ

AN EXCERPT FROM

CANNONBALL MOMENTS

ERIC A. CLAYTON

$$-1-$$

When Values and Actions Don't Match

Ignatian spirituality is built on a rather stunning premise: God of the universe desires to deal directly with us, God's beloved creations. God desires to sink deep into our stories—the mess of it all, the highs and lows and embarrassments—and take a long, loving look at what makes us tick. In fact, discovering what is important to us, what we profess to believe and value, is pivotal to understanding and accepting who we are. Naming those values and bringing them before God, realizing that it was God who put them there in the first place, is where we begin our journey in Ignatian storytelling. God created good things in creating each of us. Recognizing and claiming those values that guide us is key to recognizing and claiming our own goodness.

You are the main character of your story. And as you know from reading and watching countless stories, a character's motivation leads that character to make certain decisions and take certain actions. Your motivation springs from your values, what is important to you. So, without a firm understanding of what you value and of how those values lead you to action, your life—your story—might sputter and stall.

In this chapter, I invite you to reflect on your values. What are they? What do they point to? How do they guide your life? As you recognize those things that are important, you'll begin to see how they impact daily life, or where they fail to do so. Too often, what we think we value isn't actually translating into everyday activities. This mis-alignment between who we are and who we'd like to be is taxing on our spirit. As a result, we feel as though we're letting down ourselves and those around us. But it doesn't have to be that way.

• • •

"Do you have any change?"

We've all heard those words, I'm sure, on sidewalks and street cor-ners and outside busy marketplaces. Someone looking to us for a little help. How do we respond? With charity? Generosity? Or suspicion? Most important, how do we *want* to respond? How do we think we *should*?

I was new to the city of Baltimore, renting a room on the third floor of a classic Baltimore-style rowhome in the Charles Village neighborhood, about three miles north of downtown. I had moved to the city to start a job at Catholic Relief Services. I was to be the newest member of the team that develops the annual Lenten faith-in-action program, CRS Rice Bowl.

Despite growing up in the suburbs north of Philadelphia, I'd been to Baltimore only once or twice. I was very much *not* a city dweller. My understanding of my new hometown was a hodgepodge of facts revolving around crime and the aquarium and what I could glimpse from I-95 when en route to Washington, DC.

So it was no surprise that when two friends—fellow former vol-unteers from a Salesian mission program serving in Santa Cruz, Bolivia—came to visit me, I knew very little about the sights the city had to offer. I had one walking tour in my arsenal and proceeded to take my friends along that route. "Do you mind walking?" I asked, and they said no, and off we went. It was July in Baltimore, a hot day.

Our journey took us south of my place in Charles Village toward the Inner Harbor. We stopped for crepes just north of Penn Station, and that's where it happened: a scene now so etched into my mind, so pivotal in shaping my own forthcoming experiences of Baltimore, so common and mundane, that it was hardly noticeable to anyone but me.

The three of us approached the door, deciding that crepes would indeed be a delicious way to spend our lunch, and a man approached, down on his luck, likely without a permanent home, not unpleasant or rude. He had been lingering outside the small restaurant and, upon seeing us, set himself on a course that would collide with ours just in front of the door.

"Do you have any change?"

The question that I have grown nearly deaf to, the one that washes over me like icy water: uncomfortable for a few moments but forgotten within the hour. I lower my head and reach for the door. But my friends do not. Their heads are not lowered, their eyes not cast aside. They do not reach past the man but rather stop and greet him with a smile.

"Buddy," my one friend replied, "I don't carry any cash, but I'd be more than happy to buy you a crepe. Whichever one you'd like."

The man smiled, nodded, and said, "I'd like that. Thank you."

My other friend opened the door for him and ushered him inside, talking to him the whole time, asking his name, his story, where he lived. They bought him a savory crepe (certainly not the cheapest on the menu), and we waited with him as it was prepared.

And then, off he went, the whole encounter over in just a few minutes. I guess he liked the food, but I'll never know because he, like us, had other places to be.

Nothing revolutionary happened; every day, people buy food for those who are down on their luck. People stop and talk to those on the streets of Baltimore, New York, Philadelphia—every city in the world.

But I was dumbfounded. Embarrassed. Struck by the stark contrast between my knee-jerk reaction in front of the crepe shop and that of my friends. Encountering that man, responding in a way that didn't compute with my original intentions of purchasing a crepe and then continuing to the harbor—reverberated in my thoughts for the remainder of that day and beyond.

Not so for my companions. Their knee-jerk reaction was one of love, compassion, and fellowship. There was nothing further to think on; they did what they believed to be right. Their actions perfectly manifested what they saw to be important, just, human. And that stuck with me.

How might I reach a point where that was *my* immediate response? Because I knew that it wasn't a matter of simply buying a crepe for everyone I met on the streets. It was a matter of looking inward and challenging what I found there, digging deep to understand my own values, my sense of self, and where those values failed to manifest in the actions of my daily life.

As we endeavor to make sense of our own stories, as we grapple with what they point to about ourselves and our place in the world, a key component is articulating our values in a way that is clear, inviting, and actionable. Ignatian storytelling hinges on it.

What Made Jesus So Attractive?

Do you ever wonder if this is what drew people to Jesus? It's so easy for us to grow jaded reading the Gospels; what did Jesus *really* say that convinced people to utterly uproot their lives? Were they so unhappy that *anything* was better? I can't believe that; otherwise my faith is simply one of desperation. Did they really grasp the theological implications of Jesus' preaching? I have a hard time believing that, too, because, more often than not, we see the apostles confused by Jesus' explanation, missing the point entirely. In fact, we see that same confusion today. It seems a far cry to claim that it was solely Jesus' teaching that drew the crowds.

I have to think that what first and foremost drew people to Jesus was what he *did* and who he *was*. His knee-jerk reaction was one of love; he stopped and talked with those standing outside the crepe shop. He ushered them inside and bought them a savory crepe. And people like me stood and watched, our mouths agape because that was never what we were going to do, not in a million years.

But now, seeing it done with such love and joy, seeing it done so *naturally*—maybe that kind of instinct was achievable. Maybe it was worth hanging around people who didn't avert their eyes from a person in need, who met and held their gaze and then acted. And the person who managed to do just that—well, I might just follow that guy to see what comes next. See if he has any fishes, loaves or, better yet, wine to multiply.

What to do with all this? For me, as a Catholic, the person of Jesus Christ is central to my faith. His is the standard against which I examine my life and actions; his is the standard from which so many of my values flow. That might be true for you, too. But you might also have in mind a different spiritual figure, someone to whom you look for inspiration and encouragement, someone after whom you model your life. The values we hold are often passed down to us through our families, communities, churches, and schools.

For Saint Ignatius of Loyola and for the spirituality that bears his name, Jesus is central. An encounter with Jesus is one important way in which Ignatius encourages each of us to better understand ourselves. But that encounter isn't an academic exercise; Ignatius doesn't say we should simply study the stories of Scripture. Rather, to examine ourselves, we need to place ourselves alongside Jesus. This is a form of prayer and a way of reading Scripture that depends on our imagination. And it is through our imagination that God helps us better understand our stories: what we've been given, why it matters, and what we have to contribute.